ISBN 978-1-330-10964-9
PIBN 10028098

This book is a reproduction of an important historical work. Forgotten Books uses state-of-the-art technology to digitally reconstruct the work, preserving the original format whilst repairing imperfections present in the aged copy. In rare cases, an imperfection in the original, such as a blemish or missing page, may be replicated in our edition. We do, however, repair the vast majority of imperfections successfully; any imperfections that remain are intentionally left to preserve the state of such historical works.

1 MONTH OF
FREE
READING

at
www.ForgottenBooks.com

By purchasing this book you are eligible for one month membership to ForgottenBooks.com, giving you unlimited access to our entire collection of over 700,000 titles via our web site and mobile apps.

To claim your free month visit:
www.forgottenbooks.com/free28098

Similar Books Are Available from
www.forgottenbooks.com

Wall Shadows

A Study in American Prisons

By

Frank Tannenbaum

Author of "The Labor Movement"

With an Introduction by

Thomas Mott Osborne

G. P. Putnam's Sons

New York and London

The Knickerbocker Press

1922

by
Frank Tannenbaum

———

Made in the United States of America

To
GRACE H. CHILDS

INTRODUCTION

MANY books have been written on "Penology" or "Criminology"; most of them worthless or worse. Sometimes a writer, having previously framed some more or less plausible theory, proceeds to develop it; paying little or no attention to any facts which would disturb his theory. Another writer, having endeavored to learn the truth and accumulated a certain amount of material, writes a book as bad as the first; for his facts are incomplete or unimportant. In both cases the conclusions drawn are bound to be hopelessly inaccurate and misleading; for until a more scientific and exhaustive examination of the facts has been made, it is unsafe to theorize.

In one or the other category fall most of the books dealing with prisons. The writers do not get to the heart of their subject; for they know little of the reaction of prison life and methods upon the minds and hearts of the prisoners—these very human beings who constitute the real prison problem.

On the other hand, there are a few books by genuine men of science which are accurate and valuable; although these are less concerned, usually, with the details of prisons than with the psychology of the men before they are confined. But such a volume as William Healy's *The Individual Delinquent* is of permanent value.

For the general student the best books are these few, like Donald Lowrie's *My Life in Prison*, Al Jenning's *Through the Shadows with O. Henry* and this book of my friend, Frank Tannenbaum; books which combine a sane and healthy social point of view with an intimate knowledge of prison life.

This book differs from the others mentioned in one very important particular: it not only describes vividly the evils of existing conditions but shows the way out; it gives a constructive programme. It is well for us to

learn the facts; but if that is all, we get nowhere. In Galsworthy's powerful play, *Justice*, a certain picture of prison life is presented
with unflinching realism; but we are left without a ray of hope; no solution of the terrible
problem is even hinted at.

"Cease to lament that which thou canst not
    help,
But study help for that which thou
    lament'st."

It is good advice, always; and particularly so
about prisons.

For the past eight years some new prison
methods have been tried, based upon a principle—old in itself but never before, so far as
we know, applied to prisons. Tannenbaum
calls it "prison democracy." He has been a
careful and thorough student of the three
prisons where this principle has been utilized;
he has observed its workings, realizing the
great difficulties against which it has had
to contend; difficulties so great as to have
brought its development, at the present time,

practically to a standstill Nevertheless, what has been done once can be done again; light has been let into the dark places; so far as prison democracy has been allowed to work, it has been an unqualified success. Of course, the word "success" must be understood in a relative sense, as perfection is hardly to be expected in any human affairs. A new and "successful" system, in a manufacturing concern, is not one that is perfect, but one that turns out more and better product at the same cost or the same product at a less cost. It is exactly the same with prisons.

In connection with the operation of this new principle in prisons, much nonsense has been uttered, by thoughtless or ignorant persons, as to the danger of "coddling prisoners." No one, so far as I know, has ever advocated anything so undesirable; although the special privileges usually granted to "trusties" under the old system or under what is rather humorously called the "Honor System" (*Lucus a non lucendo*), come perilously near it. As a matter of fact, prison democracy is directly opposed to any system of "coddling," for one of its chief objects is to do away with special privileges for the undeserving.

It is highly desirable that there should be a broader realization of the fact that, for the protection of Society, a prison should be a place of punishment, but not a torture chamber; a healing hospital, but not a madhouse; an institution for education, where breakers of the law can be encouraged to become honest and useful members of society and trained toward that end. The object of the prison discipline should be to produce not good prisoners but good citizens.

A man is punished when he is branded by the condemnation of Society; he is punished when he is exiled and deprived of liberty. Such punishment it is wise to enforce, when a man has committed crime. But to give unintelligent wardens and guards, calloused and brutalized by the very system they are enforcing, the power to inflict daily torture upon their helpless victims is to defeat the very end for which prisons exist; it is to send the prisoners back into the world, at the end of their terms, seething with hatred and prepared to renew their warfare against Society, at whatever cost to themselves. Men are constantly being returned to prison, not because they like prison, but because they are trying to "get even" with the community which has tortured them and driven out of their hearts all thoughts except those of revenge.

Could there possibly be devised a more preposterous paradox?

It may be urged that all prisons do not base their discipline upon torture; that many wardens are kindly and intend to be humane; that all guards are not brutal; and in many institutions the inmates are treated with genuine consideration.

That is true; although the number of such institutions is much smaller than most people suppose. Many a kindly warden runs an institution which would surprise him if he knew what really goes on behind its walls. The "Honor System," even at its best and when it is not a poisonous fraud, does not solve the problem; for a criminal can seldom be turned from evil courses merely by kindness and the granting of special favors to those who manage to please the prison authorities. You cannot cure a thief either by flogging him, nor yet by giving him sugar-plums. Moreover, the spectacle of special favors being given to successful time-servers and hypocrites is not an edifying one; and unfortunately the rewards of the "Honor System" tend inevitably to go to the prison "rats" and "stool-pigeons"—the most hateful creatures known to man. Even the best-intentioned warden will be fooled by them.

The trouble with all these prisons, brutal or "kindly," is that there is no practical way to bring genuine grievances to the highest authority; there is no responsibility placed upon the inmates; no initiative—no training in the uses of freedom, so that the sense of what is due to the community—a man's civic duty, may be encouraged. We send a man to prison because he is deficient in that sense; then eventually set him free, after he has

INTRODUCTION

lived a longer or shorter period of time under conditions where he has never been allowed to develop or exercise that sense in any way whatever. As well train for a race or practice for a baseball game by lying for months in bed.

This paradox is as preposterous as the other.

Mr. Tannenbaum sees all sides of the prison question; and his book gives not only desirable destructive criticism of the old methods but still more valuable constructive suggestions for the new. He sets the facts about prisons clearly before us. He is a keen and intelli gent observer—one of the few who can visit such institutions and understand what he sees. He can discern matters which an ordinary visitor, or even an official investigator, misses entirely. And he dares to tell us the truth, afterwards.

It is only by knowing the full truth about the prisons that Society will ever arouse itself and be freed from the body of this death.

THOMAS MOTT OSBORNE.

AUBURN, NEW YORK,
25 December, 1921.

PREFACE

THIS book attempts to describe what happens in prison. It deals with the technique of penal administration, with the mood and the temper that pervade the prison atmosphere. This study is limited in scope. It is not concerned directly with crime and the criminal, but with the prisoner after conviction. This distinction may be somewhat artificial, but it is one we make in practice. The committed man is given into the custody of institutions that are concerned with his future rather than with his past. Once within the prison gates a new chapter begins in the life-history of the individual—and it is with this chapter that I am concerned. Our generation can do away, for good and all, with the evil done to helpless man and to society by the current penal system. It is ignorance and

PREFACE

indifference that lie at the root of the present situation and this book is written in the hope that it may help some few to take up the cause of society against our medieval prisons.

What follows reflects many experiences. It is based upon one year's imprisonment for unlawful assembly during the unemployment agitation in New York City, 1913–1914, on a voluntary confinement in Sing Sing Prison in 1916, on a study of Auburn Prison and Portsmouth Naval Prison, on a transcontinental trip of prison investigation in 1920, covering about seventy penal institutions, on contacts with prisoners, prison officials, and people interested in prison problems over a period of seven years. Specifically: I am indebted to Dr. Stagg E. Whitin for ever-ready coöperation; to Mr. Adolph Lewisohn, President of the National Committee on Prisons and Prison Labor, for contributing towards making possible the trip of prison investigation; to Miss Julia K. Jaffray for cheerfully giving her time in going over the English and for much other help; to Miss Alma Bloch for helping to get the

PREFACE

manuscript into shape; to my wife for constant helpfulness in the preparation of the
book and for reading the proof; to Dr. George
W. Kirchwey; to Professor Harry E. Barnes;
to the editor of *The Atlantic Monthly* for per-
mission to reprint the material which first
appeared in that magazine; and most of all
to the friendship of Thomas Mott Osborne,
whose work and insight have been the main-
spring of my interest in the problems of
prison administration.

F. T.

New York,
    February, 1922.

CONTENTS

Wall Shadows
A Study in American Prisons

Wall Shadows

CHAPTER I

PSYCHOLOGY OF PRISON CRUELTY

TO the uninitiated, prison cruelty seems to be a rare and isolated phenomenon. When on occasion instances of it become known and the community has its sense of decency outraged, there is generally a demand for investigation and removal of the guilty warden and keeper. With that achieved, the average citizen settles back comfortably into the old habits of life, without asking too many questions, and with the general assumption that, after all, it cannot be expected that prisons should be turned into palaces.

To him who goes into the matter more deeply, there is the added comfort, not only that the given warden has been punished for cruelty, but that there are legal and constitutional provisions against its reappearance. Our laws provide against cruel and unusual punishments, and to the average mind, with its faith in the law, this is sufficient assurance against their repetition. These facts, added to the infrequency of the publicity, strengthen the general feeling that prison brutality is a personal matter for which particular individuals are responsible.

This is the general view. But to those who are acquainted with prison organization, brutality is a constant factor—constant as the prison itself; and the publicity which upon occasion makes it known to the public has only an accidental relation to the thing itself. It is some fortunate approach on the part of an inmate to the publicity forces in the community, or some accidental trial, such as brought before the public the recent charges against Bedford, which makes it evident that brutality exists in a particular institution. It is obvious, of course, that, had it not been for the trial at which the charges of brutality at Bedford were brought in as a part of the court procedure, brutality might have existed for a long period of time without general public knowledge. I am stressing this point because it helps to carry the important fact that cruelty in prison and publicity about it are not closely related.

Historically, cruelty has always marked prison administration. We have records of brutality in prisons stretching over all written history, and including practically every nation of which we have written records. Prison brutality is both continuous and universal. Publicity, public indignation, investigation, removal of officials, and the institution of reform methods have, up to the present time, been ineffective in eliminating brutality from prison administration.

A prison is primarily a grouping of human beings involving problems of coöperation and discipline. As such, it gives room for the play of all the various emotions and instincts common to man in any other grouping. There is, however, one striking difference. This difference is that the man in the prison, just because he is shut out and away from the world, is forced, so to speak, to become a closer neighbor to himself, and therefore exhibits most of the instincts and passions, the loves and hates, the boldness and the fear, common to men, but in a more intense, more direct, and less concealed way. A prison is, in a sense, the greatest laboratory of human psychology that can be found. It compels men to live social lives—for man lives primarily by being social—under unsocial conditions, and it therefore strains to the breaking-point those things that come naturally to people in a free environment. The fact that men are more sensitive, more self-conscious, more suspicious, more intensely filled with craving, more passionately devoted in hate and in love,—just because most of these emotions are expressed in idea rather than in fact,—makes the prison a grouping of men requiring very delicate and sympathetic treatment. This is the general background which must be taken into consideration in the discussion of prison administration, and in any analysis of the forces that lead toward prison brutality. Like every human grouping, the prison group is complex, and all that one may hope to do in an analysis is to describe what seem the most important elements in the situation.

II

Our approach to the criminal is the first element in any consideration of prison brutal ity. It is obvious that somehow or other our feeling about the criminal is different from our feeling about other members of the community. We feel differently about him because we are under the impression that he is a being distinctly different from ourselves. Just why he is different, or just in what degree he is different, or whether the difference is really one that is basic in the man himself rather than in our assumption about the man, does not concern the average person. We know that he is different. This belief is common to most people, and, in general, it is shared by officials concerned with prison administration.

The elements that go to the making of this attitude may broadly be described in the following terms. The first apparent fact is that we do not ordinarily distinguish between the thing a man has done and the man himself. We tend to translate a single isolated act into a whole being, forgetting all of the man's past, with its innumerable unrecorded emotions and deeds. We make the crime and the man synonymous. In common parlance we say that the man who has stolen is a thief, and the man who has committed murder is a murderer, summarizing all of the man in terms of the single fact with which we are impressed. We thus seem to transfuse the one act which we do not like into all of the man, who may, apart from that one act, be a very lovable person, and we place him in a category distinctly outside the pale of common association and consideration. He is different. Not only different, but he is worse. Any treatment which would seem unfair and unjust for people "like ourselves" seems, even to the best of us, less unfair, less unjust, for him whom we have classified as different from and worse than ourselves.

To this may be added three other and closely related influences which tend to strengthen the feeling of difference, and to justify methods of approach which are not in common use for people not so classified. The first of these three influences is undoubtedly the feeling that the man who is in himself bad is socially undesirable. A criminal is not only a bad man in moral evaluation, but he is a bad man socially. He is not fit, to put it in colloquial terms, to associate with other people better than himself, because he may make them bad; or, in other words, he is felt to be unsocial and deserving of some method of exclusion from the community of "good" people who may suffer from contamination if he is let loose.

The second, and, to some people, a very important consideration is the fact that a man who is a criminal is not only bad, not only unsocial but also a man who has broken the law. This may not only involve a very strong emotional reaction for people to whom the law generally is a rather vague and sacred summary of all things forbidden, but it is undoubtedly a forceful fact in the life and the emotional reactions of officials, whose habitual business is centered about the enforcement of the law. A crime to them may, in fact, primarily be a violation of the law. In other words, apart from any "badness" or "unsociability" in the official immediately concerned, the breaking of the law may in itself create an emotional bias sufficient to carry a condemnation which, to ordinary people, is carried by "badness" and "social undesirability."

There is yet a third element, which, in a measure differing in different groups, contributes materially to the general conviction that the criminal is a sinful and vicious person. I refer to the general confusion in the minds of religious people between crime and sin. While not all crimes are considered sins, and not all sins are recognized as crimes, yet for most purposes there is a sufficient overlapping to add the flavor of sin and its consequences to the act of the criminal.

A criminal, to the ordinary person, is thus bad, unsocial, a violator of law, and a sinner as well. Provision is made in these four categories for the possibility of condemnation by almost every member of the community.

I have placed these considerations first, not because they are first in importance, but because they tend to define the approach toward the criminal, on the part of the officials who are to care for him during the period of punishment, expiation, or reform, or whatever you choose to consider the purpose of confinement. I say the *purpose* of confinement, because in ordinary criminal procedure confinement comes first and is the basis for punishment or reform.

III

The function of the prison is to keep the men confined. The function of the warden is to make sure that the purpose of the prison is fulfilled. He is primarily a jailer. That is *his* business. Reform, punishment, expiation for sin—these are social policies determined by social motives of which he, as jailer, becomes the agent. He is a jailer first; a reformer, a guardian, a disciplinarian, or anything else, second. Anyone who has been in prison, or who knows the prison régime, through personal contact, will corroborate this fact. The whole administrative organization of the jail is centered on keeping the men inside the walls. Men in prison are always counted. They are counted morning, noon, and night. They are counted when they rise, when they eat, when they work, and when they sleep. Like a miser hovering over his jingling coins, the warden and the keepers are constantly on edge about the safety of their charges—a safety of numbers first, of well-being afterwards.

This leads to some very important consequences. It is the core of the development of prison brutality. It is the feeding basis upon which a number of other important elements tending in the direction of brutality depend. The warden is human. Being human, he is strongly inclined to follow the path of least resistance. And the path of least resistance, in the light of the ordinary understanding of a prison warden, is to make jail-breaking hard by making the individual prisoner helpless.

One of the ways of making it easy for the warden to keep the prisoner safely, is to prevent all possibilities of collusion among the criminals. *He* knows them to be dangerous and bad men, whose interests are diametrically opposed to his. They are interested in freedom. He is interested in keeping them confined. Collusion is the greatest danger to the warden's programme. Collusion may be the means toward escape—this is the great fear of the warden. So he does what administrative interests direct under the circumstances. He attempts to isolate the individual from the group. It is easier to deal with one individual criminal than with a whole prison of criminals. And so the warden tries to achieve all the benefits of isolation, of solitary confinement, in fact, if not in form.

That this is the warden's purpose is made evident by a consideration of the facts. At Blackwell's Island, for instance, we were not allowed to have pencils or paper or thread in our cells because these might become the instruments of communication with other prisoners. The rule of silence is another illustration of the general insistence upon isolation for the individual prisoner. I am not forgetting that isolation was at one time considered a reform; that the good Quakers who introduced it were convinced of the benefits of silent communion with one's self and of meditation upon one's place and fortunes in the world. Be the cause that brought isolation into prison what it may, to the warden it is a method of administrative efficiency which has little relation to the original purpose which made isolation an ideal. But isolation, suppression, the denial of association, of communication, of friendships, are things that men cannot accept in their completeness without resistance. Men resist isolation as men resist death, because isolation, complete denial of social relations with the group, is a kind of death. It leads to a gradual disintegration of self, a distortion of the mind, and to the deterioration of all that one holds valuable in personality. Sociability becomes to the prisoner the means of sustaining a semblance of normality in an abnormal environment. It is an instinctive adjustment, and is vividly insistent just in the degree in which it is suppressed. There is no room for compromise in that isssue between the warden and the prisoner. The warden wants isolation. The men must have group-life This fact has interesting results: it makes for the growth of a definitely two-sided social organization. There is routine, discipline, the formal, methodical aspect of the prison life which centers about isolation and safety of confinement for the prisoner; and its opposite—insistent, ingenious group-organization and group-life within the sphere of isolation controlled by the administrative machine in the prison.

A visitor entering the prison sees one side—
the formal, stiff, and disciplinary side of the
prison. The prisoner knows the other. To
the visitor there exists nothing but what is
apparent. And what is apparent is formality,
uniformity, evenness, and lack of variation.
Everything looks alike.

And everything runs by the clock, the bell,
and the command of the keeper. The rest is
silence It is the disciplinarian's ideal.

But inside of this formal organization there
exists a humming life—a life of ingenuity and
association. Right under the eye of the
authorities, in spite of all the restriction
imposed, in spite of the constant watchfulness,
in spite of the insistence upon isolation, the
men manage to find a means and method of
achieving coöperation. Anyone who has been
in prison can recall a thousand ways of associ-
ating with the other prisoners. The prisoners
break every rule in the prison. They talk,
they communicate with each other, they
exchange articles and they even publish
newspapers, in spite of all the attempts at

isolation. They do it because they must. Never yet has there been a prison régime that successfully suppressed association. Not even solitary confinement does that.

In my own prison experience there are hundreds of instances which illustrate this constant violation of the rules, and the irresistible insistence upon association in some form. We were not allowed to communicate with each other, or to possess pencil or paper in our cells. But he was a poor prisoner, indeed, who had not a little pencil and a scrap of paper hidden in some crevice of the wall. As for communication, the methods are as varied as the day. For instance, one of the boys would steal a colorless ball of thread from the shops, and when stepping into the cell for the night, would slip an end to the man behind him, and that man would pass it on until it reached the end of the gallery; thrown on the floor, drawn against the wall, and tied inside a cell at each end of the gallery, it would serve as a successful means of communication throughout the night. All one had to do was to tie a slip of paper with the cell-number to the thread and give it a few jerks, and it would be passed on until it reached the designated cell.

Another instance illustrative of the unsuppressible sociability of prison life is to be found in the following personal experience. Having been placed in solitary confinement and kept there for some weeks, and being denied the right to smoke, I was regularly supplied with tobacco in spite of all rules, and in spite of all watchfulness. But more striking than this is the story of a piece of pie that was sent to my cell. One of the boys working in the keepers' mess-hall decided that I ought to have a piece of pie. Pie was served only twice a year in that prison, on very special occasions. I had the two legal pieces of pie and one illegal piece, the piece of pie stolen from the officers' mess-hall by a prisoner. He placed it in a bag and put my cell number on it. As I was in solitary confinement and he was working outside the prison proper, the piece of pie must have traveled some three days and gone through many different hands; and yet it reached me without mishap, though in a rather dried and crushed form. As pie it tasted very good; but it tasted better still because it illustrated the intense social character that is characteristic of a prison group. It must be remembered that pie was rare to all the men, and that it would have tasted equally sweet to any one of them, and yet they passed it on without eating it.

The breaking of the rules is constant, discovery frequent, and punishment follows discovery. To the warden discovery spells lack of discipline, lack of isolation, danger of collusion. It means that there are not en'ough rules and that there ought to be greater strictness. It means that the danger of collusion is serious and must be prevented. It does not mean to him that there *mus:* be association. So the rules are made more numerous, the discipline stricter, and the punishment more severe upon each discovery of a new violation. But to the prisoner punishment only intensifies the need for association. Punishment takes the form of a greater isolation, of more suppression, and for the prisoner has the result of greater discontent, more bitterness, and the greater need for friendship, for communication, and the very pleasures of attempted association, in spite of opposition. This simply means that the more rules there are, the more violations there are bound to be; and the greater the number of violations, the more numerous the rules. The greater the number of violations, the more brutal the punishments; for variety of the punishments and their intensification become, in the mind of the warden, the sole means of achieving the intimidation of the prisoner by which he rules.

Brutality leads to brutality. It hardens official and inmate alike, and makes it the ordinary and habitual method of dealing with the criminal. It adds hatred to the prisoner's reaction against the individual official, and makes the individual official more fearful, more suspicious, more constantly alert, and develops in him a reaction of hatred against the prisoner, making the need for brutality greater and its use more natural. This general consequence holds true for the whole prison. The punishment of the individual prisoner develops within the whole prison a feeling of discontent and hatred because of the natural sympathy which the prisoners feel for one whom they know to be no more guilty than themselves; and particularly because solidarity of feeling is in proportion to individual physical helplessness. This adds to the tensity of the situation in the prison, adds fuel to the discontent, and makes the need for isolation in the light of the warden's disciplinary measures more justified, brutality more normal, hatred on the part of the prison group more constant, and irritation more general.

The use of brutality on the part of the warden comes as a comparatively natural process. It becomes a matter of administrative procedure and a normal expectation on the part of the prisoner. If the warden is to punish the man for violating the rules, his field of operations is very limited.

The rules being numerous, the violations

corresponding to their number, the bitterness increasing with the rules and their violations, all tax the ingenuity of the prison officials in meting out punishments that will fit the crimes. The men in prison are already deprived of most of the privileges and rights which are ordinarily possessed by the free man. They cannot be taken away as punishment, for they are not there. The only thing at hand for the prison officials upon which to exercise their authority is the prisoner's flesh and bones. They cannot take away his liberty, for stone walls *do* a prison make. They cannot deprive him of his property. In prison most men are equally propertyless. The privileges are few, and not sufficient to satisfy the need for punishment. Nor is there that dignity and social status which among freemen may be used for purposes of control. Men in prison are not sensitive about their social standing. They have a social status all their own, it is true. But this is increased by punishment; for the punishment gives the prisoner a standing and honor in a prison community which is enjoyed among free men by a martyr in a good cause. The man must be punished. And this being the situation for which procedure must find a method—the dark cell, starvation for days at a time, beating, strait-jacketing, handcuffing, hanging to a door, or lifting from the floor become the immediate instruments at hand. They become so through the limitation of the field of punishment The habitual use of physical manhandling requires intensification to carry out the purpose of intimidation by which the prison authorities operate. In addition, the physical manhandling of the human body tends to develop an indifference to human suffering and a craving for the imposition of cruelty, which increases with the exercise of brutality.

This is the general setting for the development of other phases of cruelty and brutality. A prison, just because it centers on keeping the prisoner from escaping, succeeds not only in keeping the prisoner inside the walls, but in keeping the sun out. A prison is a dark, damp, and cheerless place.

IV

The harshness, silence, twilight, discipline
hold true, not only for the prisoner, but also
for the keeper. The keeper, too, is a prisoner.
He is there all day long, in this atmosphere
of tense emotional suppression and military
discipline, and, in addition, he is generally
there at least two nights a week when on
special duty. He is a prisoner. For him there
is little beyond the exercise of power. This
exercise is a means of escape and outlet, but it
is not a sufficient means. It does not make
the keeper a happy person. It makes him a
harsh and brutal one. The keeper subjects
the prisoners to military organization, but he
himself is subjected to a similar rule. In the
prison as he is all the time, in constant contact
with the prisoners, of whom he sees more than
of his own wife and children, his contact is
chiefly physical. He has no social relations
with them. The military discipline to which
he is subjected makes that a primary rule of
procedure on the part of the keeper. The

warden is not only afraid of collusion among the prisoners, but he is also afraid of collusion between the prisoners and the keepers. The general rule is that a keeper must not speak to a prisoner except on strictly official business, and then the words must be few and to the point. This is the ordinary rule, and the violation of it in the more strictly disciplinary prisons is followed by immediate and summary punishment.

There is, however, another reason why the keeper does not associate with the prisoner. After all *he* is a keeper, an official, a good man (at least in his own judgment). Whereas a convict is a criminal. For his own clear conscience' sake the keeper must, and does instinctively, make a sharp distinction between himself and the man whom he guards. This distinction in the mind of the keeper is absolutely essential. It is essential because we cannot brutally impose our will upon our equals and betters. We can do it only to those whom we *believe* to be inferior,—different,— and not as good as ourselves. In particular, it is *helpful* if to this feeling there is added a personal element of hatred. It all tends to make brutality easier and more natural.

The keeper, of course, does not know all this. He does not see that his hatred and contempt for the prisoner is a shield for his own conscience and a cover for his own morality. He believes the prisoner to be worse, just because he is a prisoner. This makes association between the prisoner and the keepers almost impossible, except as it expresses itself in dominance. The keeper succeeds in making a gap between himself and the prisoner, and the gap is filled by contempt.

But the prisoner is not at all ready to make the concession of inferiority. In fact, the prisoner feels that he is much better than the keeper and certainly as good as most other people in the community. This is the prisoner's morality. To him—and within his experience—there is room for reasonable conviction that all people are crooked, and that the chief distinction between himself and the others is that he has been caught and the rest are still to be caught. For if a man is not a thief he is a fool, or a poor "simp" like the keeper, who cannot make a living at anything except torturing better and smarter men than himself.

I say this feeling on the part of the prisoner is understandable in the light of his experiences. The people with whom he has associated, the police who have hounded him, the lawyers who have prosecuted or defended him, the courts instrumental in jailing him, and the keepers who guard him are, as he well knows, and have been on occasion, subject to proper influence— "proper" meaning *safe* and *remunerative* approach. That being the case, the prisoner is convinced, generally speaking, that his conviction and sentence are unjust and unfair; that he is in a way a martyr; that justice and decency are on his side; and that the poor, ignorant and simple-minded "screw" knows nothing but brutality, is simply a person beneath his own class and worthy of nothing but contempt. The gap which the keeper fills on his side is on the other side filled to its limit by the prisoner.

It is necessary fully to understand what all this means to the keeper, and its consequence upon his mental development. Most keepers enter prison as young men, long before maturity and experience have given them that larger and more sympathetic insight and understanding which come to most men as they grow older. They become the keepers of other men when they themselves are still immature and undeveloped. They are thrown into an atmosphere that tends to stifle initiative and personal activity of any kind. They are pressed from the bottom by their charges, and from the top by their superiors. They are in a vise that stifles, cramps, and destroys all spontaneity in their being, long before it has reached its full growth. Not being free men, in the sense that men are free in their work; not being able to play and laugh and associate humanly with the people with whom they are in the most constant companionship, they are not likely to be social. The suppression and the lack of personal freedom, the monotony of their existence, the constant atmosphere of hatred, suspicion, and contempt, tend to contort, to twist, and to make bitter the attitude of the keeper toward his charges. The only relation he can have with them is that of dominance, and the only pleasure and play he can get, the only exercise of initiative at his disposal, comes through the imposition of authority.   He needs pleasures, because all men need pleasures; but his pleasures become, through the prison machine, the exercise of brutality for him and pain for others.

These two elements—the exercise of authority and the resulting enjoyment of brutality— are the keynote to an understanding of the psychology of the keeper.   They are both the result of the prison organization, and both feed upon suppression.   The exercise of authority has a very peculiar influence on most men. It tends to make them domineering, abrupt, harsh, inconsiderate, and terribly opinionated. This is true to the *n*th degree in prison.   In the outside world, authority is limited by the freedom of the subject.   In the army, the soldier can always desert; in the factory, he can always quit his job. Both of these have obvious limitations, but they are not limitations that are absolute. They can be overcome in despair, in anger, or in disgust. But in prison there is no escape from authority. The authority of the keeper and the warden is absolute, and the weakness and helplessness of the prisoners are absolute. What this means is that the influence of authority tends to show itself more quickly and more con spicuously and more effectively in the prison than it does in any other organized community. The influence of domination upon those who exercise power is apparently proportioned to the weakness of those on whom the power is exercised.

Let me illustrate: I remember one day a young Irish lad was brought as a keeper into our prison. He was a small, thin-faced lad of about twenty-one. He had a coat some three sizes too large for him and a cap that reached down over his eyes. When he first made his appearance inside the walls, standing beside a long row of marching men in gray, he made a very pitiful sight. His face was a little pale, his shoulders stooping, his coat slipping down (because it was too large), his feet drawn together, a club hanging limply between the legs, his head down, his eyes on the ground. He seemed very much frightened, indeed, apparently fearing that these terrible men in gray would jump at him and bite him. But in time, as the boys who marched by smiled rather humorously at his obviously frightened appearance, he began to straighten out, to raise his eyes, to move his cap slightly upward. This change of appearance was visible from day to day. The cap moved just a little higher and he raised his eyes a little farther off the ground, his feet were a little more apart, his shoulders a little straighter, and his limp club began to swing a little more every day.

In two months young Kelly was a new man. He strutted like a peacock in his morning glory. His shy, rather frightened expression had been replaced by a harsh, domineering, rather cynical one, with just a little curl of the lower lip to the right of his mouth. He became the worst guard we had in prison. He was the youngest guard we had there. They all become a little more cautious when they become older, because they find that a prisoner may on rare occasions have a "come back"; but it takes time to learn that, and Kelly had not learned it. He became the most hated man in prison, and actually drove a gang under his charge into mutiny, so that they nearly killed him. After that Kelly was a little more cautious. He exercised his brutality on the isolated individual and was more circumspect with the group.

I have gone to this length to describe a change which took place in that boy, because I am convinced, both from observation and from what I know of prisons, that this is a fairly characteristic consequence due to the exercise of dominance within prison walls.

The prisoner gets some pleasure trying to beat the rules of the game laid down by the prison administration. These facts, combined with the morbid lonesomeness of an isolated prison community, with the intensity of the atmosphere, make the need for excitement a physical craving, at least, for some of the guards. There is thus a passion developed for cruelty in prison on the part of the keeper, which is unmistakable, and for which testimony is to be found in almost every prison memoir and the report of almost every investigation of prison cruelty. Nothing can explain the ingenious tortures, the readiness and almost the pleasure with which they are inflicted, except a strong desire in terms of emotion (rather than reasonable conviction of their utility) for their imposition. Hanging people by their wrists, handcuffing them to their doors, making them wear headcages chained around the neck, beating them with clubs, and doing other brutal things cannot be explained in terms of discipline or its effectiveness. This seems especially true when the evidence of brutality is set against the psychology of the man who has been a practitioner of that type of brutality for many years. Let me describe one instance of what was, undoubtedly, cruelty of this particular type.

In the "cooler" of Blackwell's Island we had a keeper whose business it was to look after the men in that particular place. He was a tall, lanky, slim, pale-faced person, with a bald head, except for the fringe of yellow hair hanging loosely down the back of his head. His general name in the prison was "String Beans," because he looked like a string bean, —long, lean, and crooked — except that he was yellow rather than green. His special name, the name given him by the boys in the cooler, was the "Chippie Chaser." He had a very long face, with a mouth that hung down and had no teeth in it, and eyes that were inside of his head, just a little green and rather small. He looked, as a matter of fact, the nearest thing to a copy of the proverbial devil, or what might have passed for his assistant, that I have seen outside of a picture-book.

I do not want to be unkind to the "Chippie Chaser." He had been a keeper for twenty years; practically his whole life had been passed in looking after men in their weakest and in their most brutal moments. He had been, for a long time, in charge of the confinement of the men in the cooler, or in the dark cell, before the cooler took its place, and his contact with the men was in their most helpless and least interesting moments. Confined in this little room of twenty-eight cells, locked away from the rest of the prison, his was a very dull and monotonous life. I was there fourteen days as a prisoner, but he had been there for many years as a keeper, and it is not the place where a man can keep his senses in a normal state over a long period of time. Men are put in the cooler for special discipline, and in this particular case the discipline took the form of depriving us of our beds, our clothing (except pyjamas), our food, except two slices of bread and a gill of water every twenty four hours, and of keeping us there until we were broken in spirit or succumbed to the gnawings and deterioration of a hungering body. It was his business to care for us and those like us who had been there before throughout the years. It was not a pleasant job and it did not tend to make a pleasant man.

We called him the "Chippie Chaser" because he used to chase the little birds off the window that would occasionally come there with early morning and chirp a morning song. To a man in the cooler, hungry and unwashed, with a broken body and a sick, melancholy soul, a cheering note from a little bird was a very pleasant sound. It used to refresh and lighten our burden. He knew it. That is why he chased the birds away. We knew that was why he did it, and we cursed him. But the more we cursed, the happier he seemed to be. He had developed a desire, apparently, to make us curse, to make us suffer, to exasperate us, if he could. If the bird did not provide the occasion, he would find other means to provoke us. He would stand down there on the floor and look up at us on the galleries, each one of us standing against the barred door, straining our necks to look out, and he would call us every name that he could think of. He would say things to us that cannot be said anywhere but inside a prison, where men are locked safely behind their bars. He knew a great many vile names—he had spent many years in an atmosphere where adjectives of human disrepute were a specialty. And we would say them back. But we who were hungry and weak would soon tire of this game, and, leaving the honors to him, would retire to our corners exhausted.

At times, however, not having had enough excitement, he would take a pail of cold water and spill it into the cell of one of the boys. It must be remembered that we slept on the floors, that for greater comfort the floors were hilly and the water would not all run out, that the windows were kept open, and that it was cool at night. A pail of water did not tend to add to the comfort of the situation. We responded in the only way we could—by exasperation. We howled and screeched, gritted our teeth, grabbed our buckets and slammed them against the doors, raising a desperate, maddening sound, that must have been heard in heaven. And he, standing down there looking up at the galleries where the men were foaming at the mouth with exasperation, would rub his hands, open his toothless mouth, and shout above the din of the banging buckets against the iron doors, "This is hell and I am the devil."

I take it, of course, that this is probably unusual example of cruelty But if it is different, it is different only in degree and not in kind from other types of prison cruelty. Prison organization, being what it is, leads to cruelty, and the cruelty tends to vary in form and particular emphasis with the special person who exercises it.

It must be remembered that to all of this there is to be added the fact that men who live in small cells, on poor food, without sufficient exercise or air, without the soothing influence of wife or family, in an atmosphere of suppression and extreme self-consciousness, become weak and sensitive. They tend to exaggerate the importance of little things, their nerves are on edge, and their response to imposition, even of the slightest degree, is likely to be disproportionately intense. All this only goes to make each little rule, which seems unimportant and of no consequence to an outsider, a heavy and unsupportable burden to the prisoner.

VI

There is at least one more element to be considered in the discussion of prison cruelty: the relation of the well-intentioned warden to this whole scheme of rule and discipline. The better intentioned the warden is, the more likely is he to become cruel, if he maintains the old prison organization. He generally comes into prison a comparatively ignorant man in so far as the real significance of prison organization is concerned. He knows very little about the actual workings and consequence of the prison régime. He comes, generally, with the same attitude toward the prisoner that is characteristic of most people. The men are bad and he is going to reform them. Not understanding the vicious circle of prison isolation and its results, he assumes that reform consists in the changing of a few of the more stupid rules, and that in doing so he will have laid the basis of complete regeneration of the prisoner.

But this is, of course, an idle dream. The prison cannot be changed as long as the old basis of suppression and isolation is maintained; and he finds to his dismay that the men do not reform; in spite of his good intentions, the men continue breaking the rules. He does not know that they *must* break them, so he thinks they break them because they are bad. He is a conscientious person. He means well by the community. He is outraged at a lack of gratitude on the part of the men. He becomes convinced that there are a few men who are incorrigibles, and that these few must be made a lesson of for the greater benefit of the rest So he falls back into the older ways. Were he an indifferent man instead of a reformer, he would let things go their way and not be over-sensitive about them; but just because he is sensitive, just because his intentions are good, just because he means well, he has a tendency to lose his temper, to damn the fellow who would take advantage, as he puts it, of his own good-nature, and his cruelty rises with his good intentions. I do not say he is cruel; all I say is that he means well and his cruelty is only an indirect reflection of his good intentions.

This point may seem strange, because good intentions are in themselves held, as a general rule, in such high esteem. In prison organization, however, what is important in the consideration of cruelty and its development is the fact that the old prison system exists in terms of suppression and isolation of the individual and in a denial of a social existence; and just so long as this is the major fact in prison administration, just so long is cruelty inevitable, and just so long can the cruelty phenomenon not be eliminated by a few changes in rules and regulations.

The chief merit, from this point of view, of Thomas Mott Osborne's work lies in the fact that the emphasis, instead of being upon isolation, is upon sociability; that through self-government the men are given an ever-increasing degree of inter-relationship and communication, association, group-problems and *esprit de corps*. This simply means that the prime cause of the development of the cruelty phenomenon ceases to operate, because isolation from the group ceases, and the less isolation and suppression, the less hatred, bitterness, lonesomeness, morbid self-consciousness, and moodiness; the less pressure there is upon the individual to escape, and therefore the less need there is for isolation. Just as isolation works in a vicious circle leading on to greater isolation and to more cruelty and more isolation, so its reverse leads to a lessening of the pressure upon the individual; the more sociability, the less need for cruelty and the resulting greater sociability.

Social organization in prison tends to eliminate the greater part of the evil results of the old system, to make those non-existent; and secondly, it tends to introduce a new set of consequences which emphasize the social aspects of human life, which develop initiative, self-restraint, coöperation, powers of group-activity, and all the characteristics that come from freedom of participation in the activities of the group. It brings new problems and new evils, but they are the problems and the evils of association and not those of isolation. And these new problems are the problems of democracy, and their control is to be found in the methods of democracy. Just as the old system tends to desocialize and to distort the prisoner, this new system of social organization tends to socialize the unsocial criminal, and to develop the undeveloped mind of the man who has lived—as many prisoners have—a very one-sided and incomplete life.

CHAPTER II

PRISON DEMOCRACY

IT was late at night. All were asleep except four of us—three prisoners and myself. We were smoking our pipes and drinking tea in the warden's kitchen and talking. Our conversation ranged over many things—things that are weird and fascinating when the mood of a silently creeping night has settled upon an isolated community. Suddenly I turned to one of the prisoners and said,—

"Jack, how do you like working here?"

He looked at me for a minute and replied: "Well, I like to work for the old man [Mr. Osborne]; he is a clean-cut fellow, and you always get a square deal from him; but in here I am a servant." And then, pointing through

44

the window where, in the distance, broken by a few glimmering lights, loomed the prison in outlines blacker than the night, he continued, "While there, I am a citizen."

Puzzled at his answer, I asked for an explanation; and he enlightened me with the cheerful remark: "You must be simple. Here I have to do what I am told, just like any other servant; in there we govern ourselves as free men."

A paradoxical state of mind for a convict, if one remembers the old prison system. Under the old prison system the privilege of working in the warden's house was the final mark of confidence and the most cherished of all privileges. Here, apparently, while the boys liked to work for their warden, they regretted the fact that they were not active participants in managing their own affairs as they would be if they remained in the prison proper. This sentiment was concurred in by the other men.

While thus smoking our pipes and drinking tea, I was initiated into many of the mysteries of prison democracy—one of them, the keen sense of responsibility. I was told by one of the boys in the kitchen—a fellow with a smug face and bald head, with many fanciful tattoos on his arms and chest—that this business of running a prison was no "cinch," and that the chief trouble was that some of the men who had short "bits" did not appreciate their full responsibility. At the last election, he told me, they had three tickets in the field: those who were in office and wanted to stay in; the independents who would have liked to get in; and the long-timers. I inquired for the distinctive platform of the long-timers' party.

"Well," he said, "we fellows have most to lose if this system goes wrong. We are going to stay here after the others are gone, and it is up to us to see that nothing goes wrong, because we are the *responsible* party."

I sauntered into the prison one day, and found myself in the League room, with half-a-dozen boys. An argument developed about the efficacy of the democratic method, and I found to my great surprise that democracy had staunch supporters here, stauncher than in some places that I know outside of prison. One of the men in the room—Mack, a great big fellow with broad shoulders, and a voice like that of a bull, husky and sturdy—said, with a bang on the table, "Well, be gad, I never worked in my life, but when I get through here I am going to try it, and I am going to be a labor agitator."

That was curious. I somehow could not think of Mack as a labor agitator. I said, "A labor agitator, Mack! Why in the world that?"

Mack had never been a laborer. He had been a thief all his life. He looked at me with some scorn. "Well, why not?" said he. "I tell you boys, this thing, democratic self-government, is the cure for all our troubles, and I am going to preach it when I get out."

A little later in the day I was talking to one of the men doing time—a young man, straight, well-built, blond hair, a fine sensitive face, with a good education. Technically, he never completed it, having been expelled from some half-a-dozen colleges in succession. He told me quite frankly what the trouble was. He said, "I had too much money and too little sense of proportion. I am the black sheep in my family. I was never any good, but I tell you what—when I leave this place, I am going to preach the gospel of a square deal, and I am going to do it for the rest of my life. This is the first time I have seen it applied in practice, and it works. I have found a life's job."

One day I found myself talking to a farmer lad. His sentence was two years. I wanted his opinion. He said, "Well, two years is a pretty long time for a fellow to spend any place, especially in prison; but I tell you what, I ain't so sorry that I am here. This is the greatest experience a man can have. I have learned more since I have been here than in all my other years put together, and I feel the better for it."

Sitting with two professors from Harvard, who were visiting the prison, and watching a trial where five young lads, all under twenty-one, acted as judges, while a number of witnesses were being called, I observed the young boys, one of whom, who was doing life for murder, was the presiding judge. The judge was saying, as one of the witnesses went out, in answer to an objection that there seemed to be no evidence justifying the continuance of the trial, "That is not the point. I don't think the fellow was guilty myself, but I do think some of these witnesses are lying, and the point, fellows, is, that we have got to learn to tell the truth or this darn machine won't work."

One of the professors turned to me and said, rather wistfully, "If we could only make our colleges more like this, what a different result our educational machine would achieve!"

Something strange and phenomenal had occurred just before I visited the prison. Nine motors filled with prisoners had gone to Manchester, New Hampshire, to give a play. They were practically without guard. On the way home, late at night, a blizzard developed, and in making a sharp turn in the road the two first cars, one with Mr. Osborne and the one immediately behind, took the right road, the others went astray. Mr. Osborne arrived at the prison with seven cars of prisoners missing. The other cars kept straggling in one by one as they found the way, the last one arriving about ten o'clock in the morning.

One group of prisoners had a particularly trying time of it. They ran out of gasoline, their car broke down several times, and finally burned, leaving them stranded and practically without money. In despair they waked a farmer and inquired for the county jail, planning to spend the night there and return to the prison in the morning. After making their way to a little town, from which a bus service was running in the direction of Portsmouth, and waiting until morning for the bus to start, they found that they had to borrow money to get back to the prison, as the little they had had been spent for gasoline. They all arrived safely at the prison by ten o'clock. One of them was a life-prisoner and another was doing twenty years; yet they had made no attempt to run away. Why? I don't know very well, and the men don't seem to, either. There is, however, a glimmer of explanation.

I talked to the lifer and asked him why in the world he had not run away, and he said, "What do you mean—run away? How the devil could I take the responsibility of leaving the men behind me to suffer the consequences of my having betrayed their trust in me? I went because *they* sent me, and if I had not come back they would have suffered the consequences." And then he continued without any apparent strain at all, "Why, the idea of running away never came into my head. I was sent to participate in a play and help raise some money for the boys. I enjoyed doing it, and I just came back as I was expected to—and that's all."

After a little silence he added, "We had so much trouble that night, we were so worried about how we would get back, that when we finally did come near the prison, we felt that home never looked better. It was the most natural thing for us to come back, and we did not think of anything else. The thing that I wanted most was to get a little rest, and then to tell the rest of the boys all about it."

The boy of good family mentioned above was one of those who went on this trip. He said to me, "This is an experience that I will never forget. There we were, all convicts, doing from two years to life, and free to run away, and yet no one did. What is more, I am sure if anyone had tried to do it, the others would have prevented him. There was a peculiar feeling of responsibility and of joy in carrying out the implication of this responsibility that exceeds anything I have ever believed to be possible. You see we were all free men—at least, free to run away; but our responsibility carried us back to prison, and yet you might almost say that we found our freedom in going back to confinement. Curious, isn't it? Almost ridiculous to think that men free to enjoy the possibilities of a life without restraint should return voluntarily to imprisonment just because they had a strong feeling of attachment to the men they left behind. Probably, too, there was also in our minds the knowledge that the rest would suffer if we failed them, and you know, there isn't a single one of us who regrets having come back. We feel that this experience has made the life of every one of us richer. I guess that we all came back because we were expected to and because everyone was sure that we would."

One day in Auburn, as the sun was setting over the walls, and the dim shadows of the coming night were settling down on the prison, I stood with Tony in a corner and watched the men in gray pass by on their way from the shops to their cells. Tony is a young fellow, about twenty-one, a little above medium height, broad-shouldered, well-knit, thick neck, round head, keen blue eyes, with a remarkably boyish face on which the lines of character and strength are just beginning to develop. He has a record of being one of the worst gangsters in New York City. From the age of fifteen on he dominated one of the large gangs on the upper West Side. He dominated it on the basis of personality. He proved himself the quickest, the bravest, the cleverest and the most honest—honest to his own group. He did not know any other honesty. Brought up in a family where the father was dead and the mother was poor, in an atmosphere where gangsters and professional criminals dominated his environment, he learned the fine art of being a professional criminal at an early age, and he learned it well. He knew nothing else. He had little schooling, and little experience beyond the horizon of his own immediate group, but that group he dominated. He had been tried on charges of various kinds, including murder, before this, but never convicted. Either he was too clever, or the witnesses were too much afraid of him, or, probably, he was never really "caught with the goods." Be that as it may, he was serving his first term in a state prison. Let me say that Tony was worshiped by his own group as a leader and loved as a friend.

I was standing there and talking with him when he turned to me suddenly and said,

"You know, Frank, I've got so that I can stand and 'argue' with a man."

It dawned on me slowly that he was really saying that this was the first time in his life when a difference of opinion did not involve a fight: that he could "argue" with a man when he disagreed with him, rather than fight with him.

As the men kept filing by, he said, "You know, when I first was elected top sergeant I was in a terrible fix. I wanted to punch everybody in the nose who broke the rules; but I knew that, if I punched him in the nose for breaking the rules, I'd be breaking them myself; and I couldn't do it. It was really a terrible thing. I wanted to give up the job, but I stuck it out." Then, with half a smile, "You know, I think it did me a lot of good to stick it out."

II

These are some of the evidences; I could multiply them by the hundred if there were the space, the patience, and the necessity for it.

But enough has already been said, I think, to make the reader ask the question, "What in the world is it that makes the criminal, as we know him, behave in this paradoxical fashion? These men certainly do not sound like criminals or talk like them. And if not, why not?"

Well, that is a question which this article is going to try to answer. It is a hard question to answer, and the answer is bound to be unsatisfactory.

To understand fully the significance of democratic organization in the prison, we must understand the criminal before he comes to prison. The real criminal problem is the professional criminal, the man who has, for one reason or another, accepted law-breaking as a regular method of making a living. He is *the* criminal problem. Obviously, he is not the only one who gets into jail; but any prison procedure must be judged primarily by its influence upon the professional criminal.

The men who get into prison, as I have known them inside and out, tend to divide themselves into six fairly distinct classes, which overlap, it is true, yet each of which is sufficiently distinct to stand as a group, marked off from the other groups.

The first is what might be described as the casual criminal: the man who, having once committed a crime and been discovered, is probably never going to repeat the offense; the man who is weak rather than bad, who slipped under pressure and whose sensitive consciousness and feelings of shame, as well as other influences, such as home and family, tend to keep him from repeating the act, once he has escaped, or suffered, the consequences of his first breach of the law.

The second, and a very large, part of the prison population must be classed as economic criminals. When I was at Blackwell's Island, in 1914 and 1915, the prison population of that institution increased one half. It rose from twelve hundred to eighteen hundred. What was true of that penitentiary was true of all the other criminal institutions of New York City, as I was informed by the Commissioner of

Corrections. It will be remembered that the winter of 1914-15 was one of the hardest we have had in a long time, New York City alone having some half a million men unemployed for many months. The statistics for 1919, which have just been published, show a remarkable decline in the criminal population of New York. It was a comparatively prosperous year, and there was little unemployment. This seems to indicate that economic conditions have a direct bearing on the prison population. How much more it could be reduced by improving economic conditions still further, we cannot say. But it does seem obvious that in all probability the prison population will tend to decline with the improvement in the general economic background of the men who are to-day in prison. We thus have a definite group of men who get into jail when conditions fall below a certain level, and stay out of jail when the level is raised. This group must necessarily affect all the remaining groups. The recidivist cannot be considered altogether immune from the influence of a changing economic situation.

The third group, a group much more characteristic of the workhouse and the penitentiary than of the state prison, is one that might be described as derelicts. Not all men can pass the test of industrial civilization and they break. Non-employment, sickness, accident, and other factors tend to develop irregular habits, nervous temperament, irritability, and lack of interest. They become the driftwood of the community, and some of them— one might almost say the best—drift into jail.

There was an old man in the penitentiary whom we used to call "Pop." For some twelve years he had come back every winter and left in the spring. I got to the penitentiary in February. He left in April and returned at the beginning of November, and I left him there when I was released in March of the next year.

One day I said, "Pop, why do you come back to this place so often?"

And he replied, "Well, my boy, what can

an old man do? I ain't got no home, no family; nobody wants an old man, and the work is too hard, even if I could get it. I am not a strong man any more When spring comes I go across the river to the heights, sleep in a barn, mow a lawn here and there, chop a little wood, and get by. When it gets cold again, I come back to the city, take a few good drinks, then break a window and get six months in the 'pen.' In this place I am at least sure of a bed and kept out of the cold."

"But," said I, "why don't you go to a charity institution?"

"Who—me? You must think I am a beggar. I tell you what, young fellow, I ain't. I am a self-respecting man, and I'd rather be in jail any day than in a charity home."

"Pop" is not an isolated instance. He is a type of the men and women who help to fill our city jails, and some of whom ultimately get into state prisons. They are the defeated in the struggle for life.

The fourth class is the accidental criminal: the man who runs counter to the law by accident, often the accident of good intention. In a fight that is innocent enough, a blow may be struck which has fatal consequences. Or it may be that some friend has broken the law, and in seeking to escape the police appeals for protection, for the hiding of stolen goods. The arrest of the criminal involves the well-intentioned friend, who is convicted of having received stolen goods. To this class belongs also the man who, in a passion or a fight, has struck a blow which had a worse consequence than he planned. Many men behind the bars belong to this group. Sometimes having come to jail by accident, a man continues to come through choice, a choice determined by the loss of social position, the ruin of his fortune, the acquisition of new habits, the making of new friends, the perversion of morals, the development of a feeling of hatred and revenge. A criminal record is a kind of branding of both the soul and the body. The man becomes marked, and often the police and officials help determine the destiny of the forces which an accident set in motion.

The fifth class is the definitely sick—and there are such men in prison, though not all the sick ones are there, and, in spite of the popular impression, not all who are in prison are sick. I use the word "sick" in the sense given to it by men who speak of crime as a disease, or of the criminal as diseased. There are men who are, by native capacity and content, not fit or able to live a normal life within the strained conditions of our social organization. They are often diseased, physically and mentally. These men belong in a hospital —not in a jail. But they are not so important a part of the prison population as the prison psychiatrist generally tends to indicate. The psychiatrist's conclusions will have to be checked up by a much wider analysis of the people outside of prison before his description of the characteristic features of the criminal can be accepted as conclusive.

III

This leads us to our last class, the professional criminal. He is the center of the prison problem. Recidivism is no proof of mental inferiority, of physical deformity. The evidence of those who have been in prison and who know the criminal best—the professional criminal—is contrary to any claim that would make recidivism in itself a proof of inferiority. The professional criminal is a man who has accepted crime as a profession. He has developed an aptitude for it, a liking for it. The habit, the environment, the ties of friendship, the group adhesiveness, all tend to keep him where he is. He gets there, generally speaking, through the open door of the juvenile institution. A discussion of prison democracy must be concerned with its results upon these men.

The professional criminal is peculiar in the sense that he lives a very intense emotional life He is isolated in the community. He is in it, but not of it. His social life—for all men are social—is narrow; but just because it is narrow, it is extremely tense He lives a life of warfare and has the psychology of the warrior. He is at war with the whole community. Except his very few friends in crime he trusts no one and fears everyone. Suspicion, fear, hatred, danger, desperation and passion are present in a more tense form in his life than in that of the average individual. He is restless, ill-humored, easily roused and suspicious. He lives on the brink of a deep precipice. This helps to explain his passionate hatred, his brutality, his fear, and gives poignant significance to the adage that dead men tell no tales. He holds on to his few friends with a strength and passion rare among people who live a more normal existence. His friends stand between him and discovery. They are his hold upon life, his basis of security.

Loyalty to one's group is the basic law in the underworld. Disloyalty is treason and punishable by death; for disloyalty may mean the destruction of one's friends; it may mean the hurling of the criminal over the precipice on which his whole life is built.

To the community the criminal is aggressive. To the criminal his life is one of defense primarily. The greater part of his energy, of his hopes, and of his successes, centers around escapes, around successful flight, around proper covering-up of his tracks, and around having good, loyal, and trustworthy friends to participate in his activities, who will tell no tales and keep the rest of the community outside. The criminal is thus, from his own point of view,—and I am speaking of professional criminals,—living a life of defensive warfare with the community; and the odds are heavy against him. He therefore builds up a defensive psychology against it—a psychology of boldness, bravado, and self-justification. The good criminal—which means the successful one, he who has most successfully carried through a series of depredations against the enemy, the common enemy, the public—is a hero. He is recognized as such, toasted and feasted, trusted and obeyed. But always by a little group. They live in a world of their own, a life of their own, with ideals, habits, outlook, beliefs, and associations which are peculiarly fitted to maintain the morale of the group. Loyalty, fearlessness, generosity, willingness to sacrifice one's self, perseverance in the face of prosecution, hatred of the common enemy—these are the elements that maintain the morale, but all of them are pointed against the community as a whole.

The criminal is not conscience-stricken, because his warring psychology justifies his depredations upon society. His morals center around the conviction that dishonesty (against the community) is the best policy, and more, that dishonesty is a characteristic prevailing element among other people; that the difference between the criminal who has been in jail and the rest of the community is that they are yet to be in jail.

This leads us to the criminal's background. Where does he come from? How does he acquire this peculiar concentration of the qualities characteristic of most other people, in this perverted but intense form?

The average professional criminal begins his career as a boy, often as a child; a bad boy, a naughty, turbulent, energetic, and noisy child. Some of them begin their lives of "crime" as early as the age of seven. More than twenty per cent of our criminals are under twenty-one. Raised most often as he is in poor families, in overcrowded rooms, the young boy receives little care and attention. At a very early age he generally is left to roam. The home is a place where he sleeps and has his meals—poor meals, often irregular ones and dirty. He lives in the street with other boys situated like himself, and they organize into gangs. Each little boy is striving for leadership, and fights are constant. Not living his life at home, he lives it in the street. He plays craps, collects pictures, trades, bargains, steals, avoids the policeman, hears stories of brave criminals, and being poor, finds means of increasing his expenditures for sweets, moving-pictures, and other boyish extravagances by illicit games and by being introduced to the practice of older boys. This is the setting for the average boy. What makes him into a criminal ultimately is not his gang life so much as the fact that his gang life is his *only important outlet.*

This boy finds school life rather monotonous, dull, uninteresting. The teacher is overburdened. The boy needs sympathy, love, understanding, some occupation that will give bent to his energy and discover his interest. His home brings little influence to bear upon that tendency. The school falls short of fulfilling the needs of this boy, who needs so little and yet needs it so much. He is a truant. The teacher is helpless. The mother is both helpless and hopeless. The boy is left to drift, except for the truant officer. But the truant officer, the policeman, the society for the prevention of cruelty to children, and other institutionalized elements in the community that concern themselves with this boy can generally give him everything but what he needs: he needs sympathy and understanding, and these are the two things that are rare indeed among institutionalized people and concerns.

Ultimately he gets into trouble. Some special prank, some participation in the illegal conduct of older boys, too frequent staying away from school, anything that a boy may easily do when adrift, lands him in an institution. But an institution for "incorrigible" boys is the last place for an "incorrigible" boy to be sent to. Institutions generally, regardless of their motives or objects, proceed on the basis of discipline, and the boy needs growth. Suppression does not suppress, it distorts.

One who would understand the possibility for evil, for emotional distortion, of juvenile institutions must talk at length with men who were brought up in them. He would be startled at the tales of cruelty, barbarism, neglect, and mistreatment, which, if they were not so widely corroborated by practically all men who have been brought up in such institutions, would seem unbelievable. I do not accuse of cruelty the men and women in charge of them. All one has to do is to understand the conditions under which they operate. They are but human, given to exasperation, given to becoming callous and indifferent, occupied and troubled with personal interests which make system and method essential for dealing with children. System and method imply regularity, and regularity implies, where children are concerned, inevitable deviation, difference, and friction; and to maintain regularity, discipline becomes necessary, and the limits of discipline vary very widely: they vary as widely as the human beings concerned vary; and what that means in the life of the children one need not specify, except to say that it means suppression.

The length of institutional life varies. It is, however, usually long enough to institution-alize the boy, in the sense that it tends to make him unfit for any normal and regular occupation. If he does not stay there until he is twenty-one, he very often returns two or three times to some juvenile reformatory institution before he reaches that age. He returns because his experience in the reform-atory has done nothing, generally speaking, to add to his adaptability. In the institution he has learned bad habits. I remember one "hardened" criminal saying to me, "I was sent to a juvenile institution at the age of eleven, and returned at about fifteen as a good pick-pocket. I went to a reformatory at seventeen as a pickpocket, and returned as a burglar, with all that implies in one's life and habits. As a burglar, I went to a state institution, where I acquired all the professional characteristics of the criminal and have since committed all the crimes, I suppose, which most criminals commit, and expect to end my life as a criminal."

He was a kindly old fellow, with a twinkle in his eye, and I asked him, "Dutch, how do you feel about the game, anyway?"

"Well," he replied, "my boy, when youse been in jail as long as I have, you don't feel much about what you do to other people who ain't your friends."

In the institution the boy makes a few friends, and when he is released these generally become the center of his emotional existence. He is a little more callous, a little more hardened, a little more set. He has felt his first tinge of bitterness, of hatred, of fear. He has resented brutality, and become brutal in the process, because resentment, when it breaks itself on a stone wall, hardens. Too often he comes back without a trade, without interests, with a bad name, with lurking distrust in all about him, with the police, the parole officer, and all the "good" people just a little different in their behavior toward him; and he feels different, and *feeling* different, *he is* different. He finds that he has few friends, and these few are, like himself, isolated, suspected, and persecuted. A sense of grievance binds them together. They become friends in all things. They build a loyalty that resists the encroachments of a suspicious world, and their loyalty is based both on common danger and on a sense of common grievance. There is no social consciousness, because there are no broad social connections. There is no social interest because there is no broad sense of responsibility. They are "bad," but they are bad in the sense that their good instincts have been distorted to bad motive, and not in the sense that they have no good instincts.

This then is a general background of the professional criminal, and to this background we must always remember to add the sense of constant danger and fear with which the life of the criminal is darkened.

IV

Let us see this criminal as he is when he comes to prison under the democratic organization. He has been in prison before, generally, and he knows what to expect. He finds just the opposite situation from what he has known. Instead of discipline, hard and brutal, he finds discipline based on coöperation and democratic participation. He does not understand what it means. He does not believe it, and he often, upon arrival, tries to take advantage of it.

With his background of suspicion, of hatred, of distrust, he brings with himself into prison a peculiarly aggravated sensitiveness. As a rat trapped and confined, before confinement has become a habit, gnaws at the cage and exhibits elements of desperate exasperation, so the criminal, suddenly cut off from a thousand associations, a world full of possibilities of joys and pleasures, which now seem more vivid, more keen, more essential just because they have become impossible, feels unstrung, broken, and, one might almost say, crucified. He is in no mood for the understanding of democratic organization, with its demands upon personal interest and good will. Relief, which he must have, comes slowly, and generally it comes through building a fantasy of revenge, of retaliation, of self-expression and fulfillment. It is this man who comes into prison and becomes the subject of a democratic organization. This man is the criminal problem, and prison administration must stand or fall by its effect on him.

Prison democracy is a peculiar institution. It is made up of criminals who are the citizens of this community, and yet it is not a criminal community. The men are organized on a free democratic basis, and their organization centers around problems which are peculiarly vital to the whole group. The man who originally came from a criminal community, and who under the old system was thrown into a community of criminals, now finds himself face to face, in an intensely personal way, with the grouping of men who do not operate as criminals at all; and yet their operations are of immediate consequence upon his well-being. They operate in terms of social need. Theirs are the problems of government, administration, and discipline, of education, of sanitation, nourishment, amusement—and these are not criminal problems. Like every community, this one contains its full measure of human strength and human weakness. Politics plays its part here as well as in the outside world. There are to be found intrigue, passion, jealousy, ambition, desire for leadership, for being in the limelight; there, too, is to be found the craving to serve, to be a busybody, to carry on reforms, to agitate for new things, to preach, to play, to build. It is a whole world, involving love and hatred, containing within itself some of the major problems of the outside world. There is, however, one basic difference. It must be remembered that this is an isolated community, a secluded community; that men cannot leave it at will, that what is done has an immediate influence upon the rest of the men. Government is a very personal experience in prison for every man there, because each man suffers or benefits immediately from the results of the activities of the group.

The prison community is thus essentially social. From such contact as the writer has had with prison organization he feels that it would be hard to duplicate anywhere outside of prison the social intensity and civic interest contained within a prison democracy. This paradoxical situation can probably be explained by two outstanding facts, true of the prison, but not, in their full significance, true of any other community.

The first is that life in prison is not so keenly competitive as it is in the world at large. Men are more social because the struggle for existence in the economic sense has no place in the lives of the men behind the bars. They live a life where the danger of hunger and want, where the possibilities of lack of shelter and clothing are unknown and undreamed of. There is no struggle for existence among the prisoners against each other. This means that the bitterness and disappointment, the hatred and antagonism, the selfish, competitive character of the individual is not so much in evidence. There is a kind of equality in the prison world which is almost unique. The prisoners live under the same conditions: they eat the same food, wear similar clothing. There is more unity of interest, more similarity of occupation, more consistency of habitual procedure than is to be found in the outside world. What holds true of the physical appearance of the men tends to be true also of the social aspect of their existence. The men's problems, as prisoners, are fairly similar, their interests as prisoners are more or less the same, they benefit and suffer from the common evils of prison life. They are thus bound together as men in the free outside world are not. This leads to the other aspect

77

of the prison situation which makes for socialization of the individual.

The group is so small, and their interests are so closely knit together, that the activities of any member have a direct influence on the well-being of all the others. There is not only greater proximity of physical contact, but greater dependence upon the social responsiveness of the individual. The interests of the group are so bound up with the behavior of the individual that he is under constant pressure to conform. The demand upon him to play the game honestly is almost irresistible. A man who stands out from the rest of the community by his unsocial behavior is in a more difficult situation than is the criminal in the outside world. In prison the man cannot escape the pressure of scornful, suspicious neighbors. He comes into disrepute in the community, and everyone knows all about him. He is shunned, disliked, avoided. He is scorned and sneered at, and lacks the sympathetic support of the little group which in the world outside makes the criminal's life bearable. He who will not play the game "on the level" in a prison democracy is thus an outcast who cannot avoid the most serious consequence of being an outcast—effective excommunication. The pressure for conformity in the interest of the group is thus intensified to a degree hardly imaginable. Men are caught in the vortex of a group that demands social conformity—conformity with the things and rules which are good and essential for this self-governing group. And woe to the man who will not accept the implications of social organization.

In the older prison system the honor went to the man who was the most disobedient and troublesome prisoner. Under the democratic organization he is a nuisance to the prison group and is treated as such. This fact tends to make the man who is the most insistent upon group approval—that is, the most sensitive and rebellious type under the old system —into the most social and serviceable type under democratic organization.

This does not mean that there is no competition, no difference, no deviation, no outlet for individual energy. But it is an outlet which must assume the form of emulation, of striving for greater service, rather than of anti-social behavior. The prison community has thus become one that literally compels men to take on the socialized character of the group. A prison democracy is the last place for criminals to practice crime. Conformity to the needs of the democratic group is the basis of existence, and conformity therefore becomes the rule, because the individual cannot stand up, even if he desires to do so, against the solid will of a closely knit organization.

There is another element involved, and that is the craving for play. It is an experience, new to most of them, which draws upon many potential characteristics. There is much fun, interest, and play in running for office, in administering things. There is an adventure in building a school system, as "Doc" Meyers did in Sing Sing without himself having more than an elementary education. Men who have never done anything but break laws

find a curious lot of self-expression in being
sergeant or deputy, in making or enforcing
laws. All these things have their influence.
They react upon the men who are playing the
game, and who, if they began doubtfully,
cynically, half-humorously, soon find themselves absorbed in the real problems, because
they *are* real problems. This is no longer a
criminal community. It is a community of
former criminals and present convicts, who
are functioning as independent citizens within
a certain prescribed sphere, limited by over-
shadowing walls, but within which there may
be comparative freedom. It is this community
that confronts the newcomer and, to him who
is a stranger to it, it is a perplexing and paradoxical situation.

In Sing Sing, for instance, on his arrival the
man was visited by a committee who inter-
viewed him and found out what service they
could render him. Was there anything he
wanted to learn—was there any particular job
that he could do best, or would like to do?
Was there anything that the prison organi-

zation could do to help his family? To the ordinary criminal this seemed like an attempt to "put something over" on him. It was, probably, his first experience in being offered a service without being asked for a return. Generally the newcomer, with his older psychology and outlook, would take advantage of it, and the newcomer in the prison organization was, generally speaking, a troublesome person. However, the intensity of the situation is so great, the problems so varied, the means of outlet so numerous, the area so limited, the grouping so intense, that he finds himself drawn into the vortex, one might almost say against his will.

The process by which this happens is hard to describe. It differs with different men, and varies with the varying temperament. In some cases it is cataclysmic In others it is gradual. It may happen in many ways. The man, for instance, is placed in a shop soon after he arrives in prison. He is still peevish, moody, discontented, upset, and morose. While there, somebody smiles at him genially, says a cheery word to him, or picks up something that he drops. He makes a friend. In due course he will find that there is an election coming. The whole shop is busy with interest for the competing delegates—political drumming is in the air, people are canvassing, soliciting votes, making promises; and he finds that his friend, or somebody whom his friend is interested in, is running for office, and *ipso facto* he finds himself interested. He becomes busy, anxious, excited; with a throbbing heart he stands on the edge of the group when the count is taking place; and as his friend is either defeated or successful, his heart responds with its proper beat. He is already a different man. This is the beginning of a new series of operations, of thoughts, of new interests, new ambitions.

Or perhaps his friend may have got into trouble, and he accompanies him to court; and in court he finds that he can play his due part, either as a credible witness, where his word is as good as that of any other man, or as counsel pleading the cause of his friend, or as an onlooker intensely interested in the proceedings. A vision of a new world dawns upon him. A world of social problems and responsibilities, of which he was but vaguely aware before.

Or he may like to play ball, and join the baseball team or a committee on baseball; or boxing, and join a committee on boxing; or he may have religious interests and join the Catholic committee for the proper care of the graves; or, if he is a Jew he may find himself on a committee to arrange a Passover party for the boys in prison. Anything is sufficient to make a start, and opportunities are numerous. There were some two hundred men on committees in Sing Sing during Mr. Osborne's time, about a fourth of the population serving on some committee or other, from sanitation to constitutional reform. Or he may be interested in education, going to lectures, classes, moving-pictures, or helping to teach. The particular process does not matter. What does matter is that the intensity of the social organization forces upon him social responsibility, and that the ordinary desire for con-spicuousness and play, the ordinary human interest to do one's share in the light of the ap-proval of one's fellows, is sufficient to draw him out of his hard shell, to throw back into the dimness of a receding consciousness previous thoughts, previous experiences, and previous outlook, and replace them with an altogether new set of emotions, interests, ideals.

Under the older system the prisoner had nothing to do, so he brooded upon the past and planned vengeance for the future. At present he is so busy, the interests are so various, the associations so intense, the *esprit de corps* and factional pride so constant, that he forgets, one might almost say, that he is in prison. His whole life tends to become vibrant with an altogether new set of values and a new set of experiences.

I remember sitting one night in Sing Sing with a large group of executives, board mem-bers, and other officials. It was late. The whole prison was asleep. The guards were gone, except for those outside the walls. We sat in a room smoking and talking—talking officially, because it was a meeting.

One of the boys got up and said, "Fellows, we have to look at the prison in this way. It doesn't make any difference why we are here. That is past and gone. We can't leave here when we want to, either. That is not in our power. We are here to stay. Some of us are going to stay a long time. I have twenty years. Some of the boys have life. Some of them have less than that. But we are here, and it is our business to make Sing Sing just as useful a place for the men who are here as possible, and just as interesting a place as possible. Useful to the man who is going to leave. We have got to teach him a trade and develop him into a man. Interesting and useful—at least, useful in serving those who are going to leave—must be the life of the men who are going to stay here all the time. This is going to be a hard job, I know, but we have got to do it. There is no reason why we should just rot and rot and dry up and get worse and harder and more bitter. Let's make this place into a real college for the men so that the boys who leave here will leave better and bigger men than when they came, and remember those they left behind with a good heart."

And the others approved.

This is no idle attitude of one man. The boys in Sing Sing spoke of the prison as the college for the re-making of men. The boys in Portsmouth spoke of it as the University of Portsmouth. The most interesting result of this whole business is the fact that the prisoners themselves have become prison reformers, and become so with a heart and a will, an idealism and emotional setting, which are characteristic of the true propagandist.

This newer experience, to be made permanent in the life of the criminal, must carry with it certain elements which are not directly within the power of the prison community. These men have arrived, as a result of the socializing pressure of a prison democracy, at a newer outlook, and at a newer view of life.

At least for the professional criminal, the democratic experience and its consequence are a spiritual awakening that is not to be denied. But the professional criminal, under present conditions, does not possess, generally, the means of continuing this experience when he has returned to the world from which he came. He may be a different man spiritually, but the larger community, to which he has returned, has not materially changed. Suspicion of the man who has been in prison still exists, his possibilities for work and life away from crime are not basically different from what they were before he came to prison. It is this fact which makes imperative the introduction of certain additional factors, which will tend to carry over to the world beyond the prison walls the experience and habits acquired in prison under democratic organization.

The prison must actually become a self-governing, as well as a self-sustaining community in an economic sense. It must provide the means of learning a trade as well as that of earning sufficient money for self-maintenance and the care of dependents stranded in the world outside. This is not an impossible task. There is no visible reason why scientific organization of the working and economic aspect of the prison community should not be capable of carrying full support of the individual, as well as of the group beyond the prison dependent upon the inmate for an income. It would be the means of maintaining intact such family ties as the prisoner may have had. The work, to be fully successful, must be so organized as to make possible the entrance of the criminal into an economic grouping in which he can function, and which will at the same time contain the possibilities of continuing his newer democratic experience This can apparently be done only by organizing the prison work in contact with, and under terms acceptable to, the labor unions, and thus providing for the entrance of the freed man into a labor group controlling his particular industry, and at the same time making possible the continuance of the method of democratic self-determination by participation in the problems and interests of the democratic labor organization.

CHAPTER III

SOME PRISON FACTS

"THIS is a very nice view, isn't it?" The warden was speaking—a tall broad-shouldered man in the early forties, with a rugged complexion, powerfully thick hands, and an open face with twinkling eyes. A self-made man who had risen from the rank of a guard to his present position of responsibility in one of the largest prisons in the country. He had taken me to the old prison, and pointed to the place on the wall where, twenty years before, he had started his career, pacing the wall with a rifle on his shoulder. He was proud of his newly won responsibility and conscious of it—it was a new thing.

We sat on the porch facing the prison. A

broad, quiet river flowed by the house, with a distant range of low hills, green and bright. It was a wonderful summer morning! The sun barely rising above the tree-tops, the dew still glistening in the shade, the birds singing in their varied, joyful, and madly hilarious moods, all gave the setting a cheerful atmosphere that filled every fiber with the love of life. In front of us was the prison—long gray walls partly covered with ivy, the ground round about planted with flowers, and the green grass neatly kept. The sun, driving the shadowed curtain of early dawn from the upper turrets of the inside building, made everything vibrant and happy.

We were sitting in soft chairs, smoking our pipes, looking at the prison, and talking about its manifold problems. The warden was a very good fellow, kind-hearted and well-intentioned. He was, however, a man of no learning, almost illiterate. His whole training was the training he had received in the prison; his equipment was that which the prison environment provided. A varied contact with many men who had come under his observation, combined with a natural exuberance and intelligence, with a background of goodwill that had remarkably well escaped the corroding influence of the prison atmosphere, had given him a really unusual personal equipment and power. He was telling me that he had been trained under the greatest of prison men, and considered himself a good disciple. "These men can only be treated in one way—that is, strict and steady discipline. Always be just to the men, but punish them quick and sharp when they break the rules." This completed his philosophy of life—strictness, justness, treat all men alike, and let punishment follow the breaking of a rule as the night follows the day—without exception, without fuss, constant and inevitable. He liked to talk about himself, his experiences, the men he had met, the characters he had handled, and was proud beyond words that the men considered him "square."

We sped the rising sun into the upper sky by exchanging stories and adventures. Once, years ago, he had visited New York City, and the marvel of it still dwelt with him. He told me how he had been taken down the subway, had watched the crowds on Broadway, and stood bewildered before the "crazy, shrieking, hair-tearing lunatics" in front of the Stock Exchange. The tall buildings impressed him, and the rumbling Elevated; but, most of all, the crowded East Side. "I didn't tell my wife and children half that I saw, because they wouldn't have believed me anyway; and would you think that people would live like a lot of pigs, when they could come out here in the open and free West? But man is a funny creature, ain't he? and there is no explaining him."

It was Sunday, and chapel-time came. He turned us—my wife and me—over to the assistant warden, with instructions to take us to chapel.

The assistant warden was a smaller man, stocky, a little gray, quiet, answering questions in monosyllables, and watchful. As the gates swung open, we followed him into the prison. This is one of the new structures, a model of the Auburn type—probably the best of its kind in the world. Everything was spick and span: the yard, the buildings, the halls, the brass, the marble floor—all looked shiny. It would have been difficult to find a speck of dust. In answer to a question, the assistant warden said, "We make 'em spruce 'er up." The halls were strangely silent. We could hear the echo of our steps go rumbling down the line. Nothing was visible but an occasional guard in his blue uniform and yellow buttons, standing in a corner, and saluting with his club as we went by.

The chapel, a half-circular room with something like fifteen hundred seats, was empty when we walked in and seated ourselves in the last row, the assistant warden standing at our back. The stained windows with their steel bars, the gray walls, heavy and barren, gave the whole chapel a somber and dull setting. After a few silent and restless moments, a door opened. The assistant warden nodded his head, and a second later a brazen gong struck upon the air. Suddenly, we heard the shuffling tramp, tramp, tramp of a thousand prison feet, marching on us from all sides. They came down four aisles—in single file, dressed in gray suits, their heads bare, their arms folded, shoulders stooping, bodies bent a little forward as if they were falling into the chapel rather than walking, eyes to the ground and faces turning neither to the right nor to the left. There was a listless weariness about these spiritless men, a kind of hopeless resignation, an acceptance of an unrelenting fate and a broken submission, that made the metaphor of "being broken on the wheel" seem a real, stalking, ghost-like apparition. About every twenty feet a guard in blue uniform and Sunday suit, with shoes nice and shiny, and armed with a heavy loaded cane, kept company.

As they reached the end of the aisle, the guard struck the marble floor with his loaded "butt," and the men turned half around, and filed in front of their seats. He struck the ground again, and they faced the platform. Another rap from the stick, and this sound seated the men. This continued row after row, until all the men were in their seats. When the doors were closed, the guards placed at their proper distances, facing the men, with their sticks in front of them, another rap on the ground and the hands of the men dropped to their sides. In all this time not a head had been turned, not a sound, not a whisper, not a word, nothing—not even a verbal command—had escaped the thousand men in the room. Nothing but the tramping, shuffling feet, the iron clang against the marble floor—and the stooping forms dressed in gray.

A few minutes later, a signal from the watchful master of ceremonies at our back, and a side door on the stage opened. A man dressed in black was ushered on to the platform. He was a little man, bald-headed, with thick eye-glasses and a red puggy face. As he crept across the platform, he kept pushing his hands into his pockets, pulled out a yellow paper folded many times, and began to open it. He placed the paper on the speaker's desk in front of the platform, pulled out a red handkerchief, mopped his face, cleaned and adjusted his thick glasses, hemmed and coughed a few times, stuck the paper against his nose, and began to read. He had a thin, squeaking voice, which did not reach half across the room.

It is difficult to describe the setting and the bearing of the spiritual leader of this silent and subdued flock without seeming unkind and ungenerous. I write without prejudice and without bias—but one must tell the truth. He was an ignorant man. He stumbled over the big words, would get half-way through them, only to turn back for another start. There was nothing inspiring about him, nothing cheerful, nothing interesting. It was dull, stupid, insipid. The men could not hear what he read as he read to himself, and could not understand him as he swallowed his words. The whole performance lasted some fifteen minutes, including a few prayers; and then the little man on the platform folded his yellow paper and scuttled off through the side door.

SOME PRISON FACTS

As the door closed, the first sound of the keeper's stick against the marble floor roused the men in the last row. They stood up, folded their arms, faced half-about, and began to shuffle out, followed by the next row and the next, and so until the end. Each movement was determined by the sound of the keeper's stick.

As they came out, we got a better look at the men. Most of them were young and tall, broad of shoulder and well built—men reared in the West, on farms, who had come into the cities and been dragged into the whirlpool of undercurrents that brought them to prison. Their faces were gray, their eyes sunken, dim, dull, and moody. As they noticed us sitting in the last row, their eyes shifted a little in startled surprise,—it was unusual for visitors to be seen downstairs in the chapel,—but hastily, fearfully, their eyes turned to the ground again when they noticed the little silent and grim figure at our back.

The tramp, tramp, tramp of the men could be heard as they crept down the distant halls.

Silence fell upon the chapel—a hard silence, a feeling of horror, suppression, and distortion pervaded the air and filled it with something of infinite sadness. I turned my head to look at my wife, and the tears were running down her cheeks—tears that would not be controlled. When the last sound had died down, a keeper appeared at one of the doors, nodded his head, and the guardian at our back said, "We can go now " I asked if the men had to attend chapel. He said, "Yes, prayers is good for them " I have been haunted by the chapel service. Never before had I seen anything quite so humiliating, inhuman, and sterile.

Is this a typical Sunday morning service? No, I have seen others more cheerful, less grim—places where laughter and applause could be heard, where prayers were intermingled with other things. I have seen services where there was some eloquence and a manly voice; but this picture is typical of the spiritual stagnation in prison. It is typical of the order and the discipline in prison—of the system, regularity, formalism, and, too frequently, of the silence. There is no spiritual life in the average American prison. There is no hope, no inspiration, no stimulus, no compulsion of the soul to better things. It is hard, cold, frozen, dead. This is so true, so general, so all-pervading, that one might describe the whole prison system in these few words—and I say this after seeing something like seventy penal institutions this summer.

II

The little Ford engine labored mightily as we barely climbed the steep hill to the State Reformatory at Y——. As the car reached the top of the hill, I could see, about a quarter of a mile away, a massive building with many towers, surrounded by most beautiful grounds. An uninitiated person would have taken this for some strange mediæval castle magically transplanted to this most favored spot, set off against many hills, with a clear blue sky above and mile upon mile of smiling rich fertile farmlands below. This, however, was no castle of an ancient knight—it was the stony home of many a poor lad who had been placed there for the good of his soul and the safety of the community. This, at least, is what the kindly people would have said. This was a reformatory to make bad boys good.

As I rang the bell and presented my credentials to the keeper, he looked at me doubtfully "Whom do you want?" said he, with the sharpness of a rasped temper.

"The warden," said I.

"The warden is busy."

"Yes, I know he is busy; but as I shall have to see him before I leave, you had better take these in to him now."

After a while I was presented to the warden —a tall, bony, straight-backed old man, of about sixty-five or seventy; gray, thin-lipped, sullen, and obviously displeased. As I came in, he motioned me to a chair and then turned suddenly on me. Pointing a long sharp finger in my face, he said: "I know you. You are from one of them damned reform committees who believe in coddling the prisoners. Well,

I don't. I have been in this business forty years, and know what I am talking about. You can't coddle these fellows—you can't do it. Let me tell you. I don't like these sniffling committees that come around and investigate—that come around and tell a man like me, who has been in this business forty years, how to run his prison. It is just like telling a general how to run his army. But I don't care; I will show you everything. [I was shown the sum total of nothing. But in his blustering way, he told me everything I wanted to know.] I have nothing to hide. I treat the men right; they can learn a trade, and if they are willing workers, they can earn some money—and work is good for them. This is not a bad prison. Men who are here from other prisons always tell me this is better than most. But I run this prison. No rough-neck can come here and think he is going to rough-house it. If he tries to, I fix him. *I fix him.* This is my job. A little while ago they transferred a fellow in here who said that this place was like a kindergarten, and that he would show everybody how to eat out of his hand. Well, I fixed him. He started by getting into a fight with one of my officers. I took him out into the yard, put him over a barrel, stripped him the way his father used to do, and put the cane to him—I have a good birch cane. I fixed him good and fine. No bones broken, no rough stuff, no permanent marks. It will wear off in good time. And when I had given him plenty, I riveted a seventy-pound ball and chain round his ankle and put him back in the shop from which he came. It didn't take long, only a little longer than it does to tell. But I fixed him. He has been a good dog ever since."

The warden stopped; his face relaxed a little, he looked at me as if he were well pleased, wiped his thin lips with the back of his hand, reflected a minute, and then said, "Would you believe it—I told this story to a bunch of women the other day when they asked me to speak, and they hissed me for it."

He was sincerely perplexed, and naively thought that the women must either have been "crazy," or affected by the "new-fangled" ideas.

III

This story brings me straight to the question of prison discipline in the United States. There has been so much agitation about this particular question,—and it is a crucial question,—that a survey of how things stand at present is bound to be of interest as well as significant. I must begin by saying that the agitation has mainly been outside of prison— that those affected by it were mostly people who have little or nothing to do with the prison situation. There are a few exceptions, a few indications that all the agitation has not been entirely in vain: a few changes in method, a possible reduction in the number of men punished, a relaxing of the rules a little in regard to talking and the lock-step, the abolition of such things as the strait-jacket (I am not so sure about this: rumors of its existence reached me in more than one place, but I did not actually see it), and the abolition of what was once a common practice of hanging men up by their wrists and swinging their body off the floor.

Let me introduce into this discussion of the situation the following quotation from the Detroit *News* of January 27, 1920:

"Harry L. Hulburt, warden of the prison, explained to the committee how the flogging apparatus is worked. The man to be flogged is blindfolded, hand-cuffed, and shackled at the ankles. Then he is stretched out on a long ladder, which is made to fit snugly over a barrel. The prisoner is blindfolded, the warden said, so that he will not see who is flogging him. [The warden told me, when I visited the institution, that he did it himself, as he thought that no one else should be allowed to do it.] His back is bared and a piece of stout linen cloth is placed over the bare spot. The instrument used in the paddling is a heavy strap about four inches in width, punched with small holes about an inch apart and fastened to a handle The strap is soaked in water, according to the warden, till it becomes pliable; Dr. Robert McGregor [one of the best and most conscientious prison doctors that I met on the trip], prison physician, holds the pulse of the man being flogged and gives the signal for the flogger to stop."

The article then goes on to detail three different cases of flogging. We will quote only the first.

"Thomas Shultz, boy of twenty-one years old, seven months after being sent from the insane asylum, was given 181 lashes and kept in the dungeon during the period of the flogging for nine days and fed on bread and water   November 3d, assaulted guard. For this and other minor offenses, none of them serious, he was sentenced to receive 181 lashes. November 4, he received 40 lashes. November 5th, he received 35 lashes. November 6th, he received 26 lashes. November 9th, he received 40 lashes. November 13th, he received 40 lashes. Total, 181 lashes."

Now Jackson, to which this refers, is a comparatively decent prison (I had started to use the word good; but there are no good prisons, no more than there are good diseases). If I were asked to pick the least objectionable prisons in the United States, after seeing something like seventy, I should have to include Jackson among the first ten, or possibly even among the first half-dozen. The warden is unusually intelligent, interested in his job, an advocate of the honor system, who also practises it on a large scale. He is certainly among the most humane of the wardens in the country; and, by and large, his prisoners have more freedom inside the walls than is common. I do not repeat this quotation to give it extra publicity. I repeat it to show what happens even in those prisons which are least antiquarian and hide-bound. This does not mean that all prisons have whipping. A large number still do,—more than I expected, —but old methods of punishment are still prevalent in practically all prisons.

There is hardly a prison where solitary confinement is not practiced. In some cases solitary confinement is for a few months, in some cases for a few years; and in not a few there is such a thing as permanent solitary Some prisons have a few men put away; some have as many as twenty; and in one case there are about fifty men placed in solitary for shorter or longer periods.

Why do the wardens do it? Well, they do not know what else to do. They run to the end of their ingenuity, and do that as a last resort—that is, the best of them. Some do it as a matter of common policy. I recall climbing a flight of stairs with a good-natured warden in a Western prison, and being shown a specially built courtyard with some dozen solitary cells. There were four men put away there permanently—one had been there some three years. They were not even allowed to exercise. They were not allowed to talk, they had no reading matter, they could not smoke. There had at one time been only one man in the place, and the warden permitted him to smoke; but when the others were put in, he told him not to pass any tobacco to them. This is, of course, an impossible demand. The insistence for a share of that mighty joy in solitary—a smoke—is irresistible. He did what was inevitable,—passed his tobacco and a "puff," to the other fellows,—and the war den deprived him of the privilege. "He should have obeyed what I told him if he wanted to hold on to his privilege," was the reason given.

What is true of solitary confinement is true also of the dark cell. Practically all prisons have and use dark cells. It is common to find from one to a dozen men stuck away in the dark cells, kept on bread and water—that means a little bread and about a gill of water every twenty-four hours. In most prisons—about ninety per cent—this punishment is added to by handcuffing the man to the wall or the bars of the door during the day,—that is, for a period of ten to twelve hours each day that he is in punishment,—the time varying from a few days to more than two weeks. In some institutions the handcuffs have been abolished and replaced by an iron cage made to fit the human form, which, in some cases, can be extended or contracted by the turning of a handle. A man put in the dark cell has this cage placed about him and made to fit his particular form—and it is usually made so "snug" that he has to stand straight up in the cage. He cannot bend his knees, he cannot lean against the bars, he cannot turn round; his hands are held tight against the sides of his body, and he stands straight, like a post, for a full day, on a little bread and water—and for as many days as the warden or the deputy sees fit. I was always asked to observe that they did not use handcuffs: this was the reform. Remember, a dark, pitch-black cell, with your hands pinned against your sides, your feet straight all day, unable to move or shift your ground, for ten and twelve hours a day, on bread and water, is the reform!

In one or two institutions where the cage is used,—but it is not adjustable, the man having to squeeze into the flat space as best he can,—they added the handcuffs. In one institution,—a commendable institution, as such things go, in some ways,—in one of the states that has always prided itself on being progressive, I found that they added to the dark cell the handcuffing of the man while he slept. In the particular institution I have in mind the arrangement was as follows. A bar was attached to one of the walls, and slanted down until it reached within about three inches of the floor. On this bar was a ring. At night, the board on which the man slept was placed near this slanting bar; one pair of handcuffs was put on the prisoner's wrists, another pair connected with his hands was attached to the ring on the slanting iron bar. This means that he had to lie on one side all night long, handcuffed and pressing on this board which served him as a bed.

This does not complete the list of prison punishments as they are now practiced. The underground cell is still in existence—probably not in many prisons, but I saw it in at least two different institutions. In one state prison,— an old prison, dark and damp inside,—I found a punishment cell in the cell-block. It was built underground. In the center of the hall there is an iron door flat on the ground, which one lifts sideways—like an old-type country cellar-door. It creaks on its rusty iron hinges. I climbed down a narrow flight of rickety stairs. When I got to the bottom, I had to bend double to creep into a long narrow passage. It was walled about with stone, covered with a rusty tin covering. It was not high enough to stand up in, hardly high enough for a good-sized man to sit up in. The warden above closed the door on me   I was in an absolutely pitch-black hole—long, narrow, damp, unventilated, dirty (there must be rats and vermin in it); and one has to keep a bucket for toilet purposes in that little black hole. As I came out, the warden said, naïvely, "When I put a man in here, I keep him thirty days." Let the reader imagine what that means to human flesh and blood.

I do not want to make this a chapter of horrors. Just one more case. On my way back I stopped off at a certain very well-known prison that I had heard about since childhood. For the last ten years it has been famous as one of the great reform prisons of the country. I remember seeing pictures of the warden with prisoners out on a road-gang. The article in which these pictures appeared gave a glowing account of the freedom these men had— they guarded themselves away from the prison proper, out in the hills, building roads. The state in which this prison is situated has constructed many miles of prison-built road—and, in fact, it was one of the first in the country to undertake to build roads with convict labor, without guards. When I knocked on its gates, I thrilled with expectancy. Here, at least, would I find a model prison, unique, exceptional, a pride to the state and an honor to the man who was responsible for it. In fact, I had heard that the warden was being considered for political advancement to the office of governor because of his remarkable prison record. I found a remarkable institution— remarkable for its backwardness and brutality.

The first thing that I saw as I entered the prison yard was a strange and unbelievable thing. Nine men kept going round in a circle, wheeling wheel-barrows, while a heavy chain dangled from each man's ankle. As I came nearer, I noticed in each wheelbarrow a heavy iron ball attached to the chain. In the center stood a guard; and the men kept circling about him all day long, wheeling the iron ball in their barrows, their bodies bent over, their faces sullen, their feet dragging. They did that for ninety days each, I was told by my guide. At night they carried the ball to their cells, and in the morning they carried it to the dining-room. For three months this iron ball and chain stayed riveted about their ankles —a constant companion and, I suppose, from the warden's point of view, a stimulus to better things—one of the ways of making "bad" men "good."

There, too, I found all the other characteristics of the average prison—dark cells, bread and water, solitary, handcuffs, and, in addition, a hired colored man to do whipping when that was called for—as no one else could be got to do it. This negro was never permitted in the prison yard for fear that the men might kill him. The report that I sent to the National Committee on Prisons and Prison Labor, for which I was traveling, reads as follows:

I have just visited the famous reform prison at —— and this is what I found:

Nine men going around a circle, wheeling ball and chain.

Whipping-post, with special colored man to do the task.

Dark cells.

Solitary.

Men handcuffed to the doors.

Bread and water.

No work for the men.

In addition to loss of privileges and good time, which is usual as a means of discipline.

A traveling prison chaplain had visited the institution the Sunday before I came, and made a speech to the men. In beginning his speech, he remarked upon the fame of the warden with the world abroad, and upon the fortune of the men for being under such humane treatment. Some of the men hissed. For that the moving-picture machine had been torn out from its place in the chapel, and the men were to be deprived of their weekly prison "movie" I was told also that Sunday yard-privileges had been rescinded. In telling me about it, one of the guards remarked: "We will show them [the prisoners] that this can be a real prison." I wonder what they think it is now—and what else they can add to make it one. Let this conclude the description of current disciplinary methods.

IV

The use of man by man is the basic test in the evaluation of any institution, especially one designed to make the "bad" "good," the "hard" "soft," and the "unsocial" "social." The test of a penal institution is its disciplinary methods.

The picture I have drawn is one-sided and not sufficiently comprehensive. If one desires to secure a general view of the technique of penal administration as it is at present prae-ticed, he must look at other elements of the picture. There is the problem of labor. The opportunity to keep busy during the day,—to do something that will hasten the passing hours, that will give a sense of contact with the world of reality, that will exercise one's fingers and use one's body,—this simple craving of the human organism is denied on a much larger scale than one can imagine unless he is actually brought in contact with the fact. I should say that at least one third of the prisoners in the American state prisons are unemployed. That means that in some prisons all men are working, in some practically none. and in others only a part.

The warden was an aggressive, opinionated, ignorant, and coarse individual. He had grown stout, his lower lip had hardened, his jaw jammed against his upper teeth as he talked, and at every second sentence he banged the table for emphasis, stopped, looked at you to see if you agreed with him, and if there was any doubt in his mind about this, he repeated what he had said. adding, "I am talking straight fact."

I first saw him in the evening, swinging in a soft hanging rocker on the porch, supported by small couch cushions, dressed in an immaculate white suit, with a silk handkerchief in his coat-pocket, and smoking a big cigar tilted at the proper "politician's" angle. He was round-headed, his face shiny and smooth-shaven. I felt uncomfortable sitting there in front of him and talking about the men inside. A feeling of disgust crept over me, as if he were some fat over-dressed pig—and self-assertive.

"I run this prison by psychology; if you want a lecture on psychology I will give it to you; it is all in psychology," he told me.

I begged to be excused that night. I was tired. I had driven all day; and perhaps I would enjoy it better after I saw how he managed the prison.

"All right; but remember the whole trick is psychology—it is as simple as that."

It was a typical prison—only it had an "idle house." The "idle house" is so called because it houses the idle men—men who do nothing all day long but sit on benches, crowded together, all day, every day of the week, every week of the year, and every year of their prison term—a term that may range from one year to a lifetime. It is a large bare loft. There I found four hundred men, dressed in their prison suits, sitting, all facing one way. Around the room there were keepers, seated on high stools, watching these idle men. In the morning after breakfast the men were marched to this idle house. At noon they were taken to the dining-room; after lunch they were marched back to the idle house. They were being made good by sitting. This is better than in some prisons, where the men who have nothing to do are kept in their cells. And yet—how little ingenuity it would have taken to put most of these men to work at something useful, if not remunerative. It would not have been difficult to find enough public-spirited citizens who would have provided a dozen old and broken-down automobiles and typewriters, and thus put a number of them to work taking them apart and putting them together—learning something and keeping busy, doing something. It would not have been difficult to put a number of these to studying Spanish, French, Italian—every large prison has men who would like to teach these languages and others who would like to learn them. There are a hundred ways in which these men could—at least, most of them could—have been occupied in doing something: learning how to draw, to box, to play an instrument, to typewrite—anything that would have taken the burden of eternal idleness off their hands. All it needed was a couple of days' use of the imagination. But the warden lacked the imagination. He was not really vividly conscious of the problem. When I had seen the prison and was ready to go, I asked him if he would give me that lecture on psychology, and he said with an emphatic bang on the table, "My boy, psychology is common sense."

What is true of work is true of other things. There is no imagination in the American prison field—or so little that one has to look far and wide to find it. Take the question of housing. Practically all American prisons are built on the same plan. That is the Auburn type. The best way to describe it is to begin from the outside. The first thing is the high stone wall. After you get into the prison yard made by this wall you come face to face with a large square building about five stories high. It has narrow windows, heavily barred—in some cases these windows are so narrow that it would not be possible for a man to get through them. When you enter the stone building, you find another building inside. This inside building is the cell-block, a square stone structure standing four stories high. Each tier, or floor, is divided into a large number of little cells—each cell looks like every other. Each floor is like the one below it. The cells vary in size, but not much. In the older prisons—and most of the prisons are old—the cells are about three and a half feet wide, seven feet long, and seven feet high. Some, as in Sing Sing prison, are even smaller. In the newer prisons they are larger—in some cases more than twice this size. The cells are set back to back.

The space of a cell is so small that it is inconceivable for one who has not been in it. You cannot spread your hands, you cannot lift your hand above your head, you cannot take more than three steps without hitting your toe against the wall. A cell is not larger than a good-sized grave stood on end. It is dark, half-dark, all the time. There is no window in the cell. The windows are in the outer wall and the cell is set about thirty feet away from the outer wall. The windows in this wall are generally narrow, and are always heavily barred. The sun must first get into the prison before it can get into the cell.

But the cell is not made to receive the sun. In the older prisons one half of the front facing the window is walled up. The other half has a door. In the very worst prisons, this door is completely closed at the bottom—that is, the lower half is made of solid steel To get around this, as in Sing Sing, they have drilled holes in that part. The upper half is closely netted with heavy bars, in some cases leaving only little square holes for the sun and air to get through after it finds its way into the prison. In the older cell-blocks these cells have no internal ventilation at all! All the air must come in and out through the limited space of the front door. In others, more modern, there is a ventilator in the cell—a hole going up through the wall, about six inches square. In all the old prisons the cells have no toilet system; buckets are used for toilet purposes. These buckets are generally numbered, so that each man can get his own back; but not always. As the men are put into their cells at about five in the afternoon, and taken 'out again at about six the next morning, they are in this cell-block for at least thirteen hours. Think of what it means to have eighteen hundred men in a prison under such conditions. Think of a hot July night, and picture the air on the top tier. No words can describe the pollution of the air under these conditions. Add to this the fact that, in most prisons, the men are kept in practically

all day Sunday, half a day Saturday, and, if
Monday happens to be a holiday, all day Monday, and you will have a sense of the torture
that life under these conditions imposes upon
the sensitive, and of the callousness it implies
in those who have ceased to be sensitive.

This, however, is not all. The prisons can
not be kept clean—certainly not the old
prisons,—even if there were consciousness that
this ought to be done. These old stone
structures, standing in half-darkness for a
hundred years, never having proper ventilation, never proper airing, are infected with
bugs and vermin. In my own case—and this
is typical of the old prison—the old cell-block
in Blackwell's Island was bug-ridden. In my
day there were thousands of bugs in my cell.
I struggled valiantly, constantly, and indus-
triously. But it was a hopeless fight. I had
some books, and the bugs made nests in them.
They crept over me when I slept—they made
life miserable. I am not blaming the warden
for this. I am describing a fact that we might
as well face. But the sense of sanitation is

not very keen among prison officials taken as a whole. There are a few exceptions, mostly in the new prisons.

The meaning of cell-life under these conditions cannot be conceived. I recall the day when I was first put in a cell. I stepped into a little yellow space—the walls seemed drawn together, and I halted at the door. A little yellow half-burned bulb was stuck up in the corner; there was a narrow iron cot against the wall. I heard the door behind me slam, and I felt myself cramped for space, for air, for movement. I turned quickly after the retreating officer, and called him back.

"What do you want?"

"Will—will I have to stay in this place all night?"

He laughed. "You will get used to it soon enough."

I turned back to my cell. The walls slowly retreated and made more room for me, so that I crept in and away from the door. The yellow glimmering light hurt my eyes. It was fully half an hour before I adjusted myself to the fact that I was there for the night. On my little narrow iron cot, I found two dirty blankets. I rolled them up, shoved them against the wall beneath the light, and took out a little book that I had with me.

When I came into the prison that morning, I had some books, but they were taken away. I protested that I had to have something to read—I simply had to have something. The keeper objected that it was against the rules. He looked at my books carefully, and then picked out a little paper-covered volume, which he gave me with the remark, "You can have this. We permit men to bring in anything that is religious." It was William Morris's *News from Nowhere*. The little glimmering light on the yellow page, and in a few minutes I was off in dreamland—I followed Morris's idyllic picture and perfect beings into a world where there were no prisons and no unemployed.

This happy setting was interrupted by the sobs of a boy next to my cell—he too was a newcomer. He sobbed hysterically, "My

God, what shall I do? What shall I do?" I
climbed down from my cot, knocked on the
wall of his cell, and tried to talk to him. But
he paid no attention to me. He just sobbed
and cried like a child torn from its mother,
as if his heart would break.

Finding no response, I clambered back to
my place, and was soon off in dreamland again.
I did not wake until the lights were turned out
at nine o'clock. I looked out of my cell, and
saw through the far-off window in the outer
wall a star glimmering; then, without undress-
ing, straightening my blankets, I fell asleep
and, in my sleep, dreamed of the free fields
of early childhood.

I mentioned the dirty blankets on the cot.
I used that word deliberately. It is not
uncommon for the blankets which a man gets
in prison to be dirty. They are rarely
cleaned or fumigated. One man goes out
and another comes in—receiving the blankets
the other used, without any attempt to clean
or wash them; and of course there are no
sheets. I have seen blankets so dirty that the

dust actually fell out of them when you moved them. This is not true of all prisons, but is of many.

It is not uncommon to find a prison where the men have not their own individual underwear. The underwear is sent to the laundry, and a man gets what luck will bring him: some are too long, some too short; some have been used by healthy men, some by men who were sick with contagious diseases. In some prisons the small cells have two men to a cell. There are two cots, one above the other; and these men live in this narrow cramped place— and at times the health of the men so crowded is not examined. They use the same bucket and drink out of the same cup.

Practically none of the prisons pay the men for their work. A few places make it possible for a few men to earn what might be considered a fair wage, but the mass of the prisoners earn little, in many cases nothing. Just at random: New York pays its prisoners one cent and a half a day; California and Massachusetts pay them nothing. And yet, it is asked why the men are not interested and ambitious!

Practically none of the prisons make a serious attempt to educate their prisoners. The eight grades for illiterates are in use in places—but as a rule they amount to little, both the system and the method being antiquated and the spirit poor. In only one or two places is there a real attempt to use for educational purposes the extraordinary advantages of time and control which prisons imply. San Quentin is conspicuous by the fact that it is making a real attempt in that direction. What I have said about education is true of health. Health is neglected. Here and there the fact that crime and health, both physical and mental, have a relation to each other, is gradually being recognized, but not as much or as fully as one would expect.

This rather sketchy description of American penal conditions is unfair to the exceptions —but the exceptions are few and far between. There is not a prison in the country, in so far as I have seen them, that does not fall into this general picture in one or more of its phases. Of the worst prisons, all that I have said is true. Of the better ones, some of the things I have said are true. For the casual visitor, who is taken around by a guard or by the warden, who is told all the good things and not permitted to see the bad ones, whom lack of experience and knowledge makes gullible, this may seem a startling story. If it is startling, it is not more so than the facts are.

CHAPTER IV

FACING THE PRISON PROBLEM

THE prison is a makeshift and an escape.
It is not a solution. We would hide our
sins behind its walled towers and barred windows—conceal them from ourselves. But the
prison is an open grave. It returns what we
would bury behind its gray walls. Its dark-
ness and isolation only make the sins we would
forget fester and grow, and return to stalk in
our midst and plague us more painfully than
ever. We would cover up our sins of omis-
sion—for that is what crime and criminals
largely mean in the world—by adding sins of
commission. That is imprisonment. Having
failed to straighten the lives of criminals in
childhood—to bring sweetness and light,

understanding, comfort, and good-will when it was needed, we justify our negligence by scorning the spirits we have thwarted, by breaking the bodies we have bent.

It is our attempt to escape accountability for the crimes we have committed against the men and women we call criminals. The prison is a reflex. It mirrors our hardness, our weakness, our stupidity, our selfishness, our vengeance, our brutality, our hate—everything but love and forgiveness; everything but our understanding and sympathy, everything but our intelligence and scientific knowledge.

Properly conceived, the prison should be our special means of redemption. It should be a healing ground for both the spirit and the body, where the unsocial should be socialized, the weak strengthened, the ignorant educated, the thwarted made to grow; where a kind of resetting takes place for the tasks of life, and where the strength to meet responsibility is returned to those who have lost it and awakened in those in whom it has remained dormant; a place where the joy of living and

laboring is born anew. Crime is a consequence. It is not a cause. We are responsible for its existence.

II

"The first thing is politic,—just politic,
that is it,—just politic. You get a Republi-
can and maybe he is a good sucker, and then
in a year or two you get a Democrat, and he
is a bad one, or the other way around."

One of the others interposed: "Jimmy is
right. He knows what he is talking about.
Why not make the prison like a business,
where you pick the right man and let him stay
as long as he makes good."

Here Jimmy broke in: "Let him stay—I
tell you it's all politic."

We were sitting around the large stove in
the yard of Auburn Prison, talking about
prison problems. The stove, a large field
range, was surrounded by about thirty prisoners, who were busily cooking extras. Some
were frying pancakes, some broiling steaks,
some were cooking tomato soup, and a group

of Italians was preparing spaghetti. While this was going on, others were feasting on the food already prepared, mostly seated on the ground in groups of three or four, with boxes as improvised tables. There was chattering and good-humor the circle round. It was Saturday afternoon, and the men were out in the yard—eleven hundred men. While the group I was with busied itself about the stove, others were playing handball or checkers; still others were walking about the yard, talking. Some were sitting in the shade, reading; some, congregated in groups, were throwing horse-shoes. It was a busy, quiet, cheerful crowd.

I had been let loose in the yard to visit with the men—and had found many friends. I was told by the sergeant, a tall, broad-shouldered, red-headed, round-faced fellow, with large blue eyes and a quiet voice, a man possessed of enormous reserve powers, that this stove was one of the campaign pledges which this administration had promised to the men—the prisoners' administration chosen at the last election. "We carried this pledge out, but the others have been more difficult. Our campaign pledges included the organization of an automobile class, a drawing class, and the stove. So far we have only one thing—the stove; and I say the boys enjoy it." That was quite obvious to me who had shared a large plate of spaghetti.

I had asked what, in their opinion, was the first need in prison and they had agreed: "Take politics out."

That is a good place at which to begin. Professionalize penal administration. The ordinary warden is chosen for his political allegiance; a good political reason, that, but socially no reason at all. The prison problem looked at from the administrators' point of view is a problem of education and health, complex and many-sided. It involves deep knowledge of human nature, insight into the complexities of social life, appreciation of the possibilities of personal growth and of human motives, willingness to face questions of sanitation, personal habits, hygiene, workmanship, and coöperation, in a careful, scientific, and deliberate fashion.   It is not merely a job to hold down, but a problem—or, rather, a thousand problems, requiring analysis, examination, and experiment.   A man, to be fitted for the job,—and ideally there is no such person,—approximately fitted, in spite of all the shortcomings of human weakness, must be the best-trained and best-prepared person in the field, and must have a broad basis of human sympathy and understanding.

The small henchman, from which class the average warden is recruited, is not an expert in anything,—least of all in education and health,—nor does he usually possess an imagination active enough to embrace the thousand opportunities in a prison field.   He is usually ignorant.   There is hardly a college man among the wardens of our penal institutions.   I do not insist that a college education is in itself a full requisite; but it is, by and large, better than no education at all.

Let me illustrate by describing a typical warden.   He is the head of an institution in an Eastern state, a state that prides itself upon being a great light in American cultural life. I first saw him in the death-house. He was standing near the electric chair, explaining its details to two old ladies,—small and wrinkled, gray-haired, and both over sixty. He is a tall, broad-shouldered man, with a long head, large nose, big mouth, and large gorilla hands. He was explaining in great detail how the electric chair operates. With his sagging stomach and huge bulk, he stood, a giant, beside two white-faced, white-haired pigmies. He talked in broad drawling tones and he said: "The man's head is fitted in here and strapped, the middle of it is shaved, the arms are strapped this way, and the feet here—with the trousers torn open for the current. The witnesses stand here, the reporters here, and the electrician stands here, with his hand on the switch. When all is ready and in good shape, I step forward and raise my hand,"—pointing a long finger to his breast with an expansive gesture; "the electrician pulls the switch, and bump goes the man. And if he does not go bump we do it over again."

I watched his pantomime and listened to his recitation with amazement.   A boy saying his prize piece before an admiring audience of elders could not have been more self-conscious, and better satisfied with himself.   The little, old ladies were captivated by the show, and beamed.   We walked into the prison proper, and while we were sauntering through the corridors, the warden spied a retreating figure in gray.   Stretching out his long gorilla hand, he bellowed: "Hey, Willie, come back here."

Willie was a half-witted prisoner.   He was small, round, and squatty, with a partly bald head, and a foolish grin, which stretched to his ears.   He approached bashfully, with his eyes cast down.

"Sing a song," bellowed the warden.

"I don't want to sing," appealed Willie.

"Sing, I tell you."   The warden's voice was louder still, and more authoritative.

Willie opened his mouth, and in a cracked voice began the song, "Sweetie, my sweetie."

The warden towered over him in all of his satisfied bulk   Willie had hardly begun, when a keeper in the next hall shouted, "God damn you, shut up in there!"

Willie hesitated a minute, glanced at the towering figure in front of him, and continued. The keeper, club in hand, rushed out of the next corridor, noticed the warden and the visitors, and scuttled off hastily. Later, in his office, the warden leaned back in his chair his stomach protruding over the desk, lit a big black stogie, and said with a satisfied smile, "I treat my boys right." He does, according to his lights. He gives them moving pictures once a week.

Such a situation must be made impossible. A center for the training of prison officials should be established. This school might best be situated near, or in conjunction with, some large penal institution, and no one should be appointed to a position of responsibility in prison unless he has a good collegiate education. In addition, a prison official should have taken special post-graduate courses in penal problems. No man should be a warden unless he is a certified and trained professional; just as no man is placed in charge of a hospital unless he is a graduate of a recognized medical school.

III

We must destroy the prison, root and branch. That will not solve our problem, but it will be a good beginning.

When I speak of the prison, I mean the mechanical structure, the instrument, the technique, the method which the prison involves. These must go by the board—go the way of the public stocks, the gibbet, and the rack. Obviously the penal problem will remain. That is here anyway. But the prison does not solve the penal problem—it does not even contribute to the solution. It is only an aggravation. It is a complication of the disease. It is a nuisance and a sin against our own intelligence. Let us substitute something. Almost anything will be an improvement. It cannot be worse. It cannot be more brutal and more useless. A farm, a school, a hospital, a factory, a playground—almost anything different will be better.

The suggestion for the destruction of the prison building is not revolutionary. It is not even novel. It is a practice of old standing, to keep prisoners outside of prisons; a practice not universal, but sufficiently widespread to justify the suggestion that it could be made universal without prejudice. In many prisons a number of the men are kept outside of the prison proper. Men building roads, men working on prison farms, trusties around the place, are often allowed to remain outside the walls—in some cases, hundreds of miles away from the prison, with only a guard or two. In the United States Naval Prison at Portsmouth during the war, more than half the prison population lived in wooden barracks, surrounded by a small wire fence, and with only prison inmates for guards. In the South— Mississippi, Florida, Arkansas, Louisiana—the men live so much outside the prison that the old structure is useless and an anomaly. In Arkansas, for instance. I found that the prison, built to hold six hundred men, contained thirty —most of them condemned to death; the rest were away on a farm. Prison farms are not ideal, but they are an improvement on the old cell-block. Those who argue that the old prison, with its isolated cells, its narrow windows, its high walls, its constant dampness and semi-darkness, is essential to the proper handling of the prison population are simply revealing their own incompetence, fear, lack of insight into the technique of association. The old prison is a relic of a dead past. It is a hang-over; a weight, and a hindrance against the development of new methods and new ways.

An old prejudice dies hard, and the old prison building is an ingrained prejudice carved out of stone. It is saturated with the assumption that criminals are desperate, vicious, sin-ridden, and brutal beings, who needs must be confined in buildings founded on despair and made strong against the craving for freedom; that man is incorrigible and hard, and that hardness and pain are his proper due. But all of this is mainly prejudice The men in prison are unfortunate rather than vicious, weak rather than bad. They need attention rather than neglect, understanding rather than abuse, friendship rather than isolation. Those who would redeem the community from constantly sinning against the prisoner must achieve this new attitude toward the man behind the bars The buildings are by-products of our prejudice. That is the first thing that must be battled against.

This hang-over is still so strong, that there are at present two prison buildings being constructed out of newly chiseled stone. The stone is new and white, the plans are penciled upon paper still unspoiled; but the spirit, the idea, the belief, the ideology, in which these buildings are being reared, are old, worm-ridden, petrified. But they are being constructed. Two of the largest states in the union—Pennsylvania and Illinois—are constructing them, spending millions of dollars upon a useless and condemned type of institution.

The Pennsylvania structure is simply a modern adaptation of the old cell-block type;

essentially the same thing, but with new trappings. The building in Illinois is of greater pretensions. It is reputed to be escape-proof, and is hailed as a model of modern ingenuity. As a matter of fact, it is not new at all. It is an old idea. Jeremy Bentham, in 1792, suggested it under the entertaining title of "Panopticon," and described it as "a mill for grinding rogues honest, and idle men industrious." In its modern form, it is a circular structure containing some five hundred cells. It is built so that there is air and sunshine in every one of them. Its unique feature is that one prison guard can watch the population of the whole building all of the time. Placed in the center of the structure like the hub of a wheel, raised about three stories, protected by iron walls and a closing trap-door, he can control all the cells from his point of observation.

More than that, he can look into all the cells all night and all day. The cells are made of glass and iron, and he can see straight into them, and watch each and every movement that any man makes at any time. There is to be no escape from watchfulness. That is what the guard is there for. The men are never to be by themselves. There is to be no privacy. In the old days you could get away from the hard look of the keeper for a while. You were counted frequently, it is true, but the keeper did not stand in front of your door and stare into your cell the twenty-four hours of the day. He added you up and walked on, and you could hear his footsteps go down the aisle, hear his numbering grow faint with distance, and know that for a time you were free from observation. The little trafficking, the passing of a contraband note, the exchange of a little tobacco, the quiet whispered conversation—all of these then began again and made prison life endurable. To be eternally watched is maddening. Now, there is to be no escape from the watchful, suspicious, hard look, which questions every one of your motions and is doubtful of every one of your attitudes: now the look will never waver, and the prisoner will feel a hole burning through his back even in his most serene moments. This is what we are being offered in the name of reform. And millions of dollars are being spent upon it.

A large tract of land, a big farm, small barracks, plenty of sunshine and air, and the money for education and for health, for the building of character—these are substitutes for the raising of useless and perverting stone and iron cages, where men may confine their equals for deeds which they themselves might have committed if placed in their fellows' circumstances. Professionalization of prison administration and the destruction of the present prison buildings are essentials in any programme for prison reform. But they are only beginnings.

IV

As important as these, and in some ways more fundamental, is the abandonment of the notion of punishment. Punishment is immoral. It is weak. It is useless. It is productive of evil. It engenders bitterness in those punished, hardness and self-complacency in those who impose it. To justify punishment, we develop false standards of good and bad. We caricature and distort both our victims and ourselves. They must be all black, we all white; if not, how could we impose upon others what we would not admit as applicable to our own flesh and blood. But that is not true. The difference between us and them is mainly relative and accidental; and, where real, it is a difference which may be rooted in ill health, in broken spirit, in a deformed temper, in a neglected childhood, in bad habits, in lack of education.

The penal department—the department set aside for punishment—must be eliminated from our state organization. The function of the state should be, not to punish, but to educate. The place of the penal department ought to be taken by a new bureau, dedicated to health, education, and industry, —entrusted to experts in these respective fields.

V

The prison is a great equalizer. All men are fit for it—all they need is to break the law. That done, one is stamped as a criminal, and all criminals are sent to similar places; as if all crimes were alike, and as if all men who committed them were cast in the same mold. There is practically no classification, no examination, no distribution, no elimination— break the law, and you are fit to abide with all men who have done the same, be the mood and temper as varied as the shadows that creep over the earth.

But men are not alike. They do not commit crimes for similar reasons, even if their crimes are the same. Yet often the old and the young, the weak and the strong, the normal and the erratic, the unfortunate and the vicious, the near insane and the psychopaths, all are herded together. Like the old workhouse, which contained the adolescent and the senile, the vagrant and the felon, the epileptic and the maniac, so the modern prison is an open mouth for all whom we cast aside out of the highways and byways of the world.

One of the essentials of any programme of prison reform is disintegration of the prison population. A general center for examination and classification of the men and women who are convicted must be provided, and the various groups weeded out and sent to institutions fitted for them. The imbecile, the psychopath, the maniac, the diseased, need not and should not be housed with the healthy and the normal. New York State is now building an institution for the examination and classification of men convicted of crime. Such an institution ought to find its place in the scheme of every state that undertakes to deal with penal problems in a scientific and broadly liberal spirit.

VI

With the reorganization of control and the proper grouping of the prison population should go a fundamental attempt to face the problem of health—using the word in its broadest sense. The average prison has a poorly equipped medical department. The prison is often dirty, unsanitary; the food is often poor, the ventilation old-fashioned and insufficient, and the health activities inadequate. The doctor, instead of being the independent and self-assertive individual whom the prison environment needs, is often but a tool of the warden, and remains there at his pleasure. He is usually held in general contempt by the prisoners, and has the unenviable name of Dr. Pill (because a pill is supposed to be his cure for all complaints). A distinctly new attitude to the problem must be developed. The physical condition of the men coming into the institution should be carefully examined into, as many come there with diseased bodies, with old festering sores, with bad teeth; some of the men need minor operations, others general rehabilitation; ill health often lies at the root of their failure. There are only a few institutions about which one can speak favorably in this regard—and one of these is San Quentin prison. There one finds a really definite and sincere effort to face the health problem, and a doctor in charge who might well be the boast of any institution.

VII

Work is a problem in prison. It is an unsolved problem. The prisons are not only houses of bad temper and bad humor, but they are often houses of idleness. It is no exaggeration to say that about one third of the men in prison are idle. They sit about in houses of indolence and sloth, they lie around in their cells, locked up with nothing but futility for company, or they loaf in the prison-yard. Those who work are also idling. There is no incentive to labor There is no stimulus to do a good job, there is no joy in the work done. The machinery is antiquated, the product poor, the management bad. The men do not like the work; they do not learn anything while doing it, and are literally unpaid for their labor. It is slave labor. It is not free. It is not interesting It is not remunerative. It is done under compulsion, in fear and brooding. Not more than one or two prisons are comparable in their industrial equipment to the ordinary factory where similar work is done; and the men are assigned to their tasks without regard to their aptitude, and without any attempt to discover their interests. The results are poor all around. The institutions, with a few exceptions, are not self-supporting; the men do not earn any money; the work is badly done. In some institutions the men get nothing for their labor, in some a cent and a half per day, in some two, or four cents. There are a few men in a very few institutions who earn as high as a dollar and more per day, but these are highly exceptional.

If we are ever to escape from the unfortunate condition in which our penal institutions find themselves we must reorganize the prison industries, provide work that may become the basis of a trade in the world outside, and pay the men for their work. Pay them what they earn, and make earning possible. Give some basis for zest and interest, for ambition and motive. Give them an opportunity to support their families and keep their home ties alive. There is no need to rob a man of his earning capacity just because we have found it necessary to take his freedom of movement from him. It serves no purpose but to kill ambition, to develop laziness, to engender bad habits, to destroy workmanship where it existed, to kill the joy of life, and to return men to the world less fitted to face its hardships and meet its problems than they were before being committed for violation of the law. A little imagination, a little good-will, a little interest, a little freedom from the interferences of the politician, and the whole thing could be readjusted and made to fit in a new and better way than it has ever done before; but this cannot be without a fundamental educational reorganization of the prison. The proper kind of education is one of the central needs of the prison problem.

VIII

Imprisonment is negative. It takes all. It gives nothing. It takes from the prisoners every interest, every ambition, every hope; it cuts away, with a coarse disregard for person ality, all that a man did and loved, all his work and his contacts, and gives nothing in return. It is this that makes education so essential. Education is always a challenge. It is con- structive To educate is to give something. It is to give the means to a new life, a new interest, a new ambition, a new trade, a new insight, a new technique, a new love, a drawing out of self, a forgetfulness of one's failings, and the raising of new curtains, the means to self- discovery.

All of this is a novel undertaking for the prison. Education is a charm and challenge— not only a means to a better livelihood, but also a means to a better life. It is not only what the man learns that is important, but what happens to the man while learning. One cannot acquire a new skill, develop a new interest, be brought in contact with a world of new ideas, without becoming different— essentially different—in one's reactions to the world about one, and in one's demands of it.

There is no systematic educational effort in the American prison system The warden is not often interested in education. Being himself usually unlettered, it is probably too much to expect that he should be As one goes across the country, from prison to prison, the situation is almost heartrending. Here are some hundreds and thousands of men, who have years of their lives to give to education, but are denied the opportunity. It is true, of course, that most prisons have what they call education; but that word is used to describe the teaching of the three R's to illiterates, and upon occasion an insistence that the men complete the sixth, and more rarely the eighth, grade.

But even this teaching is poorly done, in a bad spirit, and under poor organization. What one finds beyond that is little enough. Education is often frowned upon, and made impossible. I remember one poor fellow telling me, with tears in his eyes, that he wanted to take a course in mechanical drafting from a correspondence school, but this was not allowed because a man could write only one letter a month, and that on a single sheet of paper. It is true, of course, that here and there one finds a few prisoners taking correspondence courses, but it is rare, and always much boasted of.

There is only one institution which has undertaken to face the problem seriously, and that is San Quentin. San Quentin is not a model prison. It has many faults. But its health and educational activities are real contributions to the prison problem. There I found a genuine interest in education, and an ambition to attempt the experiment of turning the prison into an educational institution. Some nine hundred men were registered in eleven hundred individual courses. The chaplain who is in charge of the work, has, with the coöperation of the University of California, made a genuine beginning of what is the most interesting and promising educational experiment in the American prisons. He has succeeded in building up a staff of inmates as assistants, and the University provides an

occasional lecturer.   The work was in full pro-
gress, and gave evidence of much enthusiasm.

This undertaking is valuable and significant,
but it does not meet the needs of education
in prisons.   The courses were mostly cultural
in character.   History, economics, literature,
mathematics, and similar topics—with short-
hand and typewriting well to the front, and
one course in mechanics.   All this, of course,
has its value.   But the men in prison are not
essentially adapted to academic training, and
can make little use of it.

What the men need, and what the prison
needs, is something different, and something
new in educational work—at least so far as the
prison is concerned.   The prison must be
viewed as a community—with manifold community problems and with much community
work.   Such a turning of attention upon the
prison as a community, provides a wide field
of educational activity and interest, and would
lay the foundation of trades and knowledge
that could be used in the work-a-day world
when the men were freed.

Work in prison should be made to have educational value. There are the problems of sanitation, of heating, of feeding, of clothing the men. All kinds of work find a place in the prison, from upkeep to production; and prison education must be so organized as to provide a professional interest in and knowledge of the work done. There is, for instance, kitchen work. It is difficult to maintain an efficient and interested kitchen staff. It does not appeal to the men. Most of them are not going to follow this profession after they are released. The cooking is bad and the sanitation worse.

Professionalize the work. Give it an intellectual and scientific setting. Organize a course in dietetics in connection with your kitchen; teach the value and composition of the various foods, their preparation, the whole question of health as bound up with food, the origins of the various foods, their market—in fact, give all that can be given which has a bearing upon the problem and method of feeding many people. Give all the science, from chemistry to physiology, which would go to make the work interesting, intelligible, and valuable as a means of livelihood outside; and, not to be forgotten, which would go to increase the efficiency, the interest, and the willingness of the men in prison. This same method could be followed in all work done in the prison; and no work which cannot be done with this kind of educational programme should be permitted.

There is the problem of lighting a prison. Make the electrical apparatus and the electrical needs of the prison the basis for an extensive course in electrical engineering. Give the men all that is possible about the subject—give them something for their time. There are the men working in the boiler room —give them such knowledge of physics, of heating methods, of coal, of the properties of steam, of the organization of the heating-plant, of boiler construction, of the mechanics involved, as would help them to a good job in the world outside, and make them interested and efficient men inside.

Take such a prosaic thing as the making of clothing, of shoes. Organize a course in designing; in the properties of cloth, or leather; in the nature of modern machinery; in the character of the clothing market; in the organization of the industry; permit individuals to specialize, as their aptitude makes it possible.

Almost every prison has a chicken farm of some kind. Organize in connection with that, a course in poultry—the feeding, raising, marketing, and care of chickens; the construction of coops; the proper care of incubators, and their types; the diseases of poultry and their prevention. This could be done with the farm as a whole, and with fruit-raising. The piggery could be put to similar use. The dairy could be made the basis of a course in dairy farming, the care of cows, how to judge them—everything connected with the problem of a scientific dairy could and should be given.

Again, there are such things as painting the prison or the barns—the nature of paints, their proper mixing, their chemistry, the estimates involved, and all other things essential. The same method could be followed with road-construction: grading, machinery, materials used, and other aspects of road-work could be studied in the course dealing with this subject.

Such an educational system would return tenfold in the efficiency resulting, in the interest and good-humor, and the new outlook upon life which it would create. A new technique involves a re-orienting of the whole individual to his own and other people's problems. Such training should be compulsory,—just as the work is,—and should be considered a part of the work.

All this, of course, does not involve the elimination of the purely cultural courses, but it does involve an emphasis upon this particular type of education and an attempt to give ordinary prison-work the educational value which it lacks. It must be remembered that the men are there for many years, and that there is the time and the opportunity for such an undertaking, lacking in the world outside.

And if the men are in prison because of lack of adaptability, such education would prove an efficacious means to readjustment, to the developing of character, and to raising the level of initiative and the increase of insight into the problems of the world.

IX

It is not possible in a single article to cover all of the needs for a proper prison technique. At best, one can suggest only the most important things. But, before closing, I wish to discuss three more points that should go into any prison programme: The indeterminate sentence, parole, and self-government.

The indeterminate sentence is essential to prison reform. It is stupid to assume that a flat sentence is a proper way of settling the question of crime. As one boy put it to me, "Why don't they gas us, or something. They give a young kid of nineteen or twenty, fifteen, twenty, and sometimes thirty years. What for? What good does it do? Do they think we will be better for having rotted for a lifetime?

Do they think that we will be reformed! If they want to get rid of us, why don't they just gas us and put us out of the way!"

The indeterminate sentence suggests that a man sentenced to prison be released, not when an artificial time-period, imposed by a judge in some passing humor, has expired, but when he is fit to return to society. Such a basis of release, to be made possible, would call for the adoption of all the suggestions made in this paper, and, in particular, the educational system. That might well become the best, and certainly an essential, basis of judgment in any release under an indeterminate sentence law. I am speaking of the absolute indeterminate sentence as against the minimum—maximum sentence now in vogue in many states.

With this, or before this can become a universal practice, there should be a much broader development of the parole system. There are many men in prison who ought not remain there a day longer—who ought never to have been sent there. Their release is impossible because of the arbitrary demands of the law, that a certain legal infraction carry a particular time-punishment. In going across the country, I asked the wardens with whom I came in contact the same question: "Your present parole system proves that somewhere between 70 and 95 per cent of the men paroled 'make good' You parole about 10 per cent of your inmates each year. In five years you will have paroled 50 per cent. If, instead of waiting five years, you released that 50 per cent right away, would you have just as good results?"

The answer was, almost always, "Yes, I think we would."

As I proceeded, I became bolder and, when I found a particularly intelligent warden, I asked him the same question, but made it 75 rather than 50 per cent. He reflected a few seconds, and said, "I think 75 per cent is pretty high, but I feel sure that we could release 50 per cent of our inmates on parole to-night, and get just as good results as we are getting with the 10 per cent that we release during the year." On the testimony of the prison wardens themselves, one half of the prison population could be released without proportionately endangering the safety of the community. And every man kept in prison a day longer than the interests of the community demand means an unnecessary cruelty against a helpless individual.

This leads to my last point: community organization. Community organization in prison is Mr. Osborne's contribution to the subject of prison reform. It is fundamental. Without it no real solution of the problem is possible. It is the one essential element in any programme, and without it all reforms are bound to result in failure. There is a peculiar drive in prison administration under autocratic management, which leads to abuse, to cruelty, to indifference. Self-government is necessary for the men and for the officials. The testimony of such an experienced warden as Mr. Moyer, former Warden of Atlanta and the present Superintendent of the District of Columbia Penal System, that self-government is a great help to the prison administrator, cannot be disregarded. And anyone who has seen it in practice knows its value as a means toward spiritual growth for the men.

Those who deny this, who look upon it as a fad, who help to destroy Mr. Osborne's work, do not understand what they are doing. In Portsmouth prison the Mutual Welfare League, the instrument for self-government, was discarded, despite the fact that for four years under Mr. Osborne, and later under Commodore Wadhams, self-government had proved a blessing to the men confined, an experience and education which started many an inmate upon a better and happier life than could have been possible under any other penal system. Those who destroy this new movement are of the past; their minds are prejudiced and their hearts filled with fear. For it is fear and prejudice that stand aghast at attempted community organization in prison; at attempts to give to the men behind the bars a part of the responsibility for solving the manifold problems which a prison imposes, and which have never been solved so well, so humanely, so cleanly, as under Mr. Osborne's administration.

There is nothing in the programme here outlined which the present generation cannot accomplish if only it has the will and the interest needed. It is one way to redeem our community from continuing perverse and unsocial procedure against men and women who are more sinned against than sinning.

A Selection from the
Catalogue of

G. P. PUTNAM'S SONS

**Complete Catalogues sent
on application**

LABOR MOVEMENT
Its Conservative Functions and Social Consequences

By

FRANK TANNENBAUM

Octavo

What Eminent Authorities Say of Mr. Tannenbaum's Book:

"It is novel, interesting, and brilliantly written, and emphasizes the point of view which is in great danger of being misapprehended. I have the highest regard for the ability and the attainments of the author, and I cordially recommend the book."—*Professor Edwin R. A. Seligman.*

"I know of no one who tackles the problem in the way he does; I know of no person so peculiarly fitted to deal with the labor movement both from within and from without; I know of no work of the sort that is so broad in vision and so stimulating in suggestion. . . . The book is temperate and fair-minded; and the discussion (even the dissent) which it will evoke, will be worth while."
Professor Carlton J. H. Hayes.

"A genuine contribution to the subject."
Professor Benj. B. Kendrick.

"So far as I know, this is the first effort by an American student to interpret the American labor movement in the light of the policy and performance of American trade unions. This is sadly needed. In England it was done early and well by the Webbs."—*Professor Leo Wolman.*

G. P. PUTNAM'S SONS

NEW YORK   LONDON

CPSIA information can be obtained at www.ICGtesting.com
Printed in the USA
BVOW06s1002021115

425243BV00032B/388/P